1920
1930
Volume III

TIME
LIFE
BOOKS
®

This Fabulous Century

1920 1930

Volume III

By the Editors of TIME-LIFE BOOKS

Time-Life Books, New York

TIME-LIFE BOOKS

FOUNDER
Henry R. Luce 1898-1967

Editor-in-Chief: Hedley Donovan
Chairman of the Board: Andrew Heiskell
President: James R. Shepley
Chairman, Executive Committee: James A. Linen
Editorial Director: Louis Banks

Vice Chairman: Roy E. Larsen

EDITOR
Jerry Korn

Executive Editor
A. B. C. Whipple

Planning Director
Oliver E. Allen

Text Director   *Art Director*
Martin Mann   Sheldon Cotler

Chief of Research
Beatrice T. Dobie

Director of Photography
Melvin L. Scott

Assistant Text Directors:
Ogden Tanner, Diana Hirsh
Assistant Art Director: Arnold C. Holeywell
Assistant Chief of Research: Martha T. Goolrick

PUBLISHER
Joan D. Manley

General Manager: John D. McSweeney
Business Manager: John Steven Maxwell
Sales Director: Carl G. Jaeger
Promotion Director: Paul R. Stewart
Public Relations Director: Nicholas Benton

THIS FABULOUS CENTURY

SERIES EDITOR: Ezra Bowen
Picture Editor: Mary Y. Steinbauer
Designer: John R. Martinez
Assistant Designer: Jean L. Morein
Staff Writers: Leon Greene, Sam Halper, Anne
Horan, Gerald Simons, David S. Thomson,
Bryce S. Walker, Edmund White
Researchers: Alice Baker, Nancy Cabasin, Terry
Drucker, Elizabeth Evans, Helen Greenway,
Marcia A. Gillespie, Helen M. Hinkle, Carol
Isenberg, Nancy J. Jacobsen
Design Assistant: Anne B. Landry

EDITORIAL PRODUCTION
Production Editor: Douglas B. Graham
Quality Director: Robert L. Young
Assistant: James J. Cox
Copy Staff: Rosalind Stubenberg,
Susan B. Galloway, Florence Keith
Picture Department: Dolores A. Littles,
Barbara S. Simon

The following individuals and departments of Time Inc. gave valuable aid in the preparation of this book: Editorial Production, Norman Airey, Nicholas Costino Jr.; Library, Peter Draz; Picture Collection, Doris O'Neil; Photographic Laboratory, George Karas; TIME-LIFE News Service, Murray J. Gart; Correspondents Jane Beatty (Philadelphia); Ron Berquist (Chicago); Jim Bready (Baltimore); Patricia Chandler (New Orleans); Jane Estes (Seattle); Juliane Greenwalt (Detroit); Blanche Hardin (Denver); Frank Leeming Jr. (St. Louis); Holland McCombs (Dallas); Gayle Miller (Washington, D.C.); Jane Rieker (Miami); Gayle Rosenberg (Los Angeles); Rod Van Every (Milwaukee); Nelson Wadsworth (Salt Lake City); Sue Wymelenberg (Boston).

Contents

America
1920-1930

Fifth Avenue at 42nd Street, New York, 1926.

Coeds at Omaha's Creighton University, 1924.

Chow line at a Texas Baptist encampment, 1921.

Chicago police arrest bathers for indecent exposure, 1922.

Tea dance at Miami's new Nautilus Hotel, 1925.

Fingernail inspection in Louisville, about 1920.

The D.A.R. dedicates a marker in a Nebraska cornfield, 1927.

Children's fashion contest in Harlem, about 1928.

Crowds gather after a bomb blasted Wall Street in 1920, killing 30.

The old President (left) rides with the new to the 1921 inauguration.

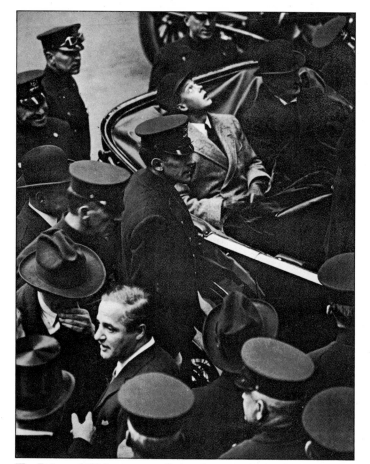

The Prince of Wales gazes at Gotham's towers during his 1924 visit.

Marie of Romania is greeted by New York's Mayor Walker in 1926.

Introducing talkies in 1927, Al Jolson vocalizes in "The Jazz Singer."

The irate parents glare past the happy pair in "Abie's Irish Rose."

The Quest for Normalcy

America's present need is not heroics but healing; not nostrums but normalcy; not revolution but restoration; not surgery but serenity. WARREN G. HARDING, 1920

On the crisp, clear morning of March 4, 1921, in Washington, D.C., a parade of stately touring cars drove along Pennsylvania Avenue from the White House to the Capitol building. At the procession's head, in the rear seat of a Pierce-Arrow, sat two men in top hats and velvet-collared chesterfields *(opposite, top right):* Woodrow Wilson, the outgoing President of the United States, and his successor, Warren Gamaliel Harding. In the inaugural ceremony that was about to take place, the country was changing not only its chief executive, but its mood, its outlook and its aspirations.

No two leaders could have been less alike. Wilson, prim and scholarly-looking, was a man whose era had passed. In the name of idealism, he had led America through a devastating war in Europe. In peacetime he had crusaded for reform at home and had admonished the nation to take up new responsibilities of world leadership. But Americans had grown tired of responsibilities and crusades. In the election of 1920 the country rejected Wilson's policies, leaving him embittered and broken, his health and his dreams shattered.

The abandonment of Wilson reflected a change in the nation's basic attitudes. The promised millennium of world peace and democracy still had not arrived. After the slaughter and the privations of the war, people felt that their efforts had not really been worth it. Other moral certainties of earlier years also were coming under attack. Disturbing notions, such as the sexual theories of Sigmund Freud and the barely comprehensible discoveries of Albert Einstein, were eroding the sanctity of family life and challenging man's pre-eminence in the scheme of things. With its old values going sour, the nation was self-conscious and unsure of itself. America seemed suspended between the innocence and security of childhood and the wisdom and poise of maturity.

Many Americans reacted to the unsettling new elements of the era by affecting a kind of romantic cynicism. Like the youthful F. Scott Fitzgerald, they professed "to find all Gods dead, all wars fought, all faiths in man shaken." Others simply refused to worry themselves about anything but their own business; almost everybody agreed that the problems of the world were too confusing, and had best be ignored.

The man America turned to at the start of the decade seemed to offer a happy escape from the rigors of problem solving. Like the nation that elected him, he was something of an adolescent. Warren Harding never allowed the problems of high office to mar his congenital good humor. "The most notable quality of Harding was the sweetness of his nature," wrote a contemporary. "He gave out love." That Harding was not a particularly able man apparently bothered no one. The only fault anyone seemed to find with him was a fondness for what he called "bloviating," or windy speechmaking—a practice described by William Gibbs McAdoo, a former Secretary of the Treasury, as giving "the impression of an army of pompous phrases moving over the landscape in search of an idea."

In the Presidential car on that March morning in 1921, Harding strained to make conversation with the sick man next to him. He told Wilson about his fondness for pet animals. He said that some day he would like to own a pet elephant. Wilson, in a thin attempt at humor, said he hoped the elephant would not be a white one.

For Harding the Presidency was just that. The new President suffered from a vital flaw: he refused to face responsibility. One of the problems that eluded his attention was the fact that his cronies were systematically robbing the public till. During his Presidency one close friend in a government post was revealed to be involved in graft, and two others committed suicide to escape prosecution. His Secretary of the Interior, Albert Fall, was implicated in an oil scandal, and rumors were circulating about his Attorney General, Harry Daugherty, who had mysteriously banked $75,000 while he was earning a salary of only $12,000. Shaken by these betrayals, Harding died in office on August 2, 1923, of a heart attack.

Despite all this, Harding's policy of governmental inactivity had been popular, and his successor, Calvin Coolidge, tried to carry it a step further. To make sure he did nothing to rock the boat, Coolidge spent from two to four hours of every working day taking a nap.

In the freewheeling mood of the decade, strong government seemed not only boring, but unnecessary. The nation's troubles, people felt, were somehow solving themselves, without official interference. Though business had slumped a bit at the beginning of the decade, the economy soon began to boom. Overblown rumors of a Communist conspiracy had aroused fears just after the war; but the last incident of any importance had been in September 1920, when an anarchist bomb had exploded on Wall Street opposite the plutocratic Morgan bank.

Instead of problems, Americans in the '20s craved excitement. Almost anything, no matter how trivial or preposterous, seemed to give it to them—a gory murder in the tabloids, a world championship boxing match, a royal visit. In 1924, when Britain's young Prince of Wales made a pleasure jaunt to the United States, the nation went wild with excitement. Similar enthusiasm was lavished on Queen Marie of Romania when she toured the country in 1926, accompanied by a retinue of press agents.

The opening of "Abie's Irish Rose"—one of the longest-lived, most widely panned plays in U.S. theater history— drew from critic Robert Benchley of the old "Life" magazine the review excerpted below. As the play went on and on, the exasperated Benchley tried desperately to steer readers away from it in his magazine's weekly column of drama offerings. A selection of these follow-up critiques appears on pages 25 and 26. (The original review followed another about a play called "The Rotters"—up to that moment "just about the worst show of the season.")

On the night following the presentation of "The Rotters," residents of Broadway were startled by the sound of horses' hoofs clattering up the famous thoroughfare. Rushing to their windows they saw a man, in Colonial costume, riding a bay mare from whose eyes flashed fire. The man was shouting as he rode: " 'The Rotters' is no longer the worst play in town! 'Abie's Irish Rose' has just opened!"

"Abie's Irish Rose" is the kind of play in which a Jewish boy, wanting to marry an Irish girl named Rosemary Murphy, tells his orthodox father that her name is Rosie Murphesky, and the wedding proceeds. Any further information will be furnished at the old offices of "Puck," the comic weekly which flourished in the '90s and is no longer in existence.

ROBERT C. BENCHLEY, *LIFE*, 1922

When a lanky, soft-spoken youth named Charles Lindbergh made the first solo airplane flight nonstop from New York to Paris in 1927, America pulled out the stops. As he was escorted up Broadway, jubilant crowds showered the returning hero with 1,800 tons of shredded paper.

A spirit of frivolity seized the country. Women began cutting their hair at ear level and hemming their dresses to knee level. Otherwise respectable citizens began dancing the Charleston, carrying hip flasks and visiting speak-

easies. H. L. Mencken, caustic critic of contemporary whims and vagaries, was once asked why, if he found so much to complain about in America, he bothered to live there. "Why do men go to zoos?" he replied.

The unrestrained hedonism of the decade fed on its own momentum. The Prohibition amendment that became law in 1920 had turned the simple pleasure of sipping a tot of whiskey into a federal offense—and many Americans began regularly and unremorsefully to violate the law. While many were seeking escape from responsibility through bathtub gin, others went to the movies. Here was a world where fantasy and flamboyance galloped unchecked. Settings became ever more extravagant, costumes more exotic, sex more emphatic. By the time Hollywood had supplemented sex with the additional inducement of sound, movies had become a way of life for most of America. The first talkie arrived in 1927 in the form of a film called *The Jazz Singer*, starring Al Jolson in blackface. By 1930 the silents had flickered out, and the talkies were pulling in 90 million viewers a week.

The decade also sought escape in the theater. While some playwrights, such as Eugene O'Neill, were writing intense dramas of deep psychological import, most of the nation's theater-goers preferred lighter fare. Comedy, or a kind of smiling-through-the-tears sentimentality, remained the order of the day. One Broadway show, a hearts-and-flowers romance between a Jewish boy and an Irish colleen, was so unabashedly mawkish that critics hated it *(see boxes)* and audiences professed to be embarrassed by it. Yet *Abie's Irish Rose* ran for 2,327 performances over a period of five years and five months, setting a record for theatrical longevity.

Buoying up the pleasures and frivolities of the '20s was the most spectacular economic boom the country had ever seen. If some Americans felt disillusionment over politics or religion, they could find solace in a new faith based on the omnipotence of the dollar. Materialism flourished like an evangelical cult, as the country placed its faith in the supreme importance of automobiles and washing machines. If not everyone was growing rich, people felt that the chances for becoming rich were getting better every day. During the period from 1921 to 1929, the gross national product soared from $74 billion to $104.4 billion. The buying power of wages for a skilled laborer swelled 50 per cent from 1913 to 1927. Bricklayers' wives began to spruce up their wardrobes with silk stockings and white gloves. Their husbands began riding about in Niagara Blue roadsters or Arabian Sand phaetons.

Beneath all the self-conscious gaiety of the '20s, serious problems lurked; life and its concerns did not go away

just because people were not paying attention. The prosperity and excitement that millions of Americans enjoyed left millions of others untouched. Many of the country's people—especially in rural areas—had never tasted a drop of bathtub gin, never played mah-jongg, never heard of Freud, knew of jazz babies and flappers only through the movies, read their Bible faithfully and believed every word the Gospel said. In thousands of small communities, from the cotton fields of the South to the wheat-covered plains of the Middle West, life went on as usual.

In some places it was worse than usual. Large sections of the economy had failed to recover from the "temporary" economic downturn of 1920-1921. The index of farm prices, which had stood at 205 at the beginning of 1920, had plummeted to 116 a year later and by 1927 had only returned to 131. Western lumbermen, New England textile workers and coal miners in Pennsylvania and West Virginia suffered nearly as badly. Worst of all was the plight of the Negro sharecropper in the South, who lived in virtual economic slavery. He gave up to 75 per cent of all

> *May 7, 1925 Abie's Irish Rose—If this runs until May 22 it will have broken the record held by "Lightnin'" for length of run. We are as nervous as a witch. Suppose it should have to close by May 21!*
> *May 28, 1925 Abie's Irish Rose—Now let's just make this fourth year the biggest and best of all.*
>
> ROBERT C. BENCHLEY, *LIFE*

the cotton or tobacco he raised to his white landlord. His income from the remainder amounted to less than $350 a year. On top of everything else, the Negro suffered from a resurgence of race hatred. During the first half of the decade there was a rebirth of the Ku Klux Klan, a white supremacist organization dating from Reconstruction days; Klan membership swelled to four million by 1924.

Amid the general indifference of the decade, only a few instances of social injustice managed to ruffle the conscience of the nation—or, more accurately, of a small but vocal part of the nation. The chief *cause célèbre* was the Sacco-Vanzetti case. On May 5, 1920, two professed anarchists named Nicola Sacco and Bartolomeo Vanzetti were arrested on charges that they had killed two men in a payroll robbery at South Braintree, Massachusetts. Both men were immigrants, neither could speak English very well and both had avoided the World War I draft on ideological grounds. To some aroused Americans the evidence against Sacco and Vanzetti seemed inconclusive, and many were convinced that the two men were the victims of raw prejudice because they were foreigners, radicals and draft dodgers. Nevertheless, after seven

> *October 14, 1926 Abie's Irish Rose—Abie's Irish Rose—Abie's Irish Rose. That takes care of it up to November 4th.*
>
> ROBERT C. BENCHLEY, *LIFE*

years of litigation and uproar the men were executed.

In short, serious matters persisted in intruding on the fun and frolic of the '20s. Even among the most frivolous there was an air of desperation. "What most distinguishes the generation who have approached maturity since the debacle of idealism at the end of the War," said Walter Lippmann, "is not their rebellion against the religion and the moral code of their parents, but their disillusionment with their own rebellion. It is common for young men and women to rebel, but that they should rebel sadly and without faith in their rebellion, that they should distrust the new freedom no less than the old certainties—that is something of a novelty." Behind the bright surfaces of the '20s, its carnival of public events, the glitter of its prosperity, its love of enjoyment, lay an abiding sense of futility. The axiom of the decade was "Eat, drink and be merry," but it had its corollary: "For tomorrow we die."

On October 24, 1929, came the event that (though few realized it then) brought the decade to a close. On that

> *May 19, 1927 Abie's Irish Rose—Five years old on Sunday. Somehow we've lost interest by now.*
> *November 3, 1927 Abie's Irish Rose—There is a play by another name supposed to be at this theater now, but you can't fool us. We know what it really is.*
>
> ROBERT C. BENCHLEY, *LIFE*

day the stock market, which had been wavering for weeks, suddenly plunged. It was only the beginning *(page 128)*. The Great Depression had begun; in the rigors of this disaster, the strength of America would be sorely tried.

Air general Billy Mitchell (left) is tried for insubordination (page 223).

Hero Charles A. Lindbergh is welcomed to Broadway by ticker tape.

The resurgent Ku Klux Klan demonstrates its strength in 1925 by staging a 40,000-man parade down Pennsylvania Avenue in Washington.

Nicola Sacco (left) and Bartolomeo Vanzetti await their trial in 1920.

Mobsters' bodies sprawl in a garage on February 14, 1929 (page 175).

Flaming Youth

Boys and girls in California brazenly puff on cigarettes.

An Age of Sheiks and Shebas

They're all desperadoes, these kids, all of them with any life in their veins; the girls as well as the boys; maybe more than the boys.

FLAMING YOUTH BY WARNER FABIAN

The '20s were an exciting—and perhaps a frightening—time to be young. It was the era of the First Youth Rebellion. Once boys had tried to be paragons of gallantry, industry and idealism; girls had aspired to seem modest and maidenly. Now all that had changed. "The uncertainties of 1919 were over," F. Scott Fitzgerald wrote. "America was going on the greatest, gaudiest spree in history."

In a refrain that would be heard again and again in later generations, John F. Carter Jr. wrote in the *Atlantic Monthly:* "I would like to observe that the older generation had certainly pretty well ruined this world before passing it on to us. They give us this Thing, knocked to pieces, leaky, red-hot, threatening to blow up; and then they are surprised that we don't accept it with the same enthusiasm with which they received it."

The new questioning of their elders' authority, combined with the relative affluence of the decade, spawned a breed of youngsters who claimed to be hard-boiled, heavy-drinking and daring—and sometimes were. The girls in particular seemed to have changed. Skirts were shorter than ever before. Cloche hats, silk stockings, fake jewelry, bobbed hair replaced the osprey plumes, hobble skirts and flowing tresses of yesteryear. The advent of Pro-

hibition made clandestine drinking an appealing game; women took up the sport alongside men. They also took up smoking; sales of cigarettes doubled during the decade.

Morals were undergoing a revolution. More and more college-age boys owned automobiles—and were parking them on dark roads to "neck" with their dates. Suddenly Freud's name was on everyone's lips. One writer complained: "Today, let some ingenue venture, 'I had the queerest dream—' and all at once we see a crowd, a host of parlor analysts. The obliging interpreters listen,—though this is hardly necessary,—look wise, and at the end exclaim 'Aha! That means *sex!* You have a sex-complex!' "

Inevitably, the daring clothes, the scandalous dances and sensual jazz, the late-night parties and cynical opinions of the youth drew the wrath of many members of the older generation. "The situation," declared a Southern Baptist publication, "causes grave concern on the part of all who have the ideals at heart of purity and home life and the stability of our American civilization."

But America's young people didn't care. They went right on in their heedless, happy way, adopting the outrageous fashions shown on the following pages, and singing, "In the mean time, in between time, ain't we got fun?"

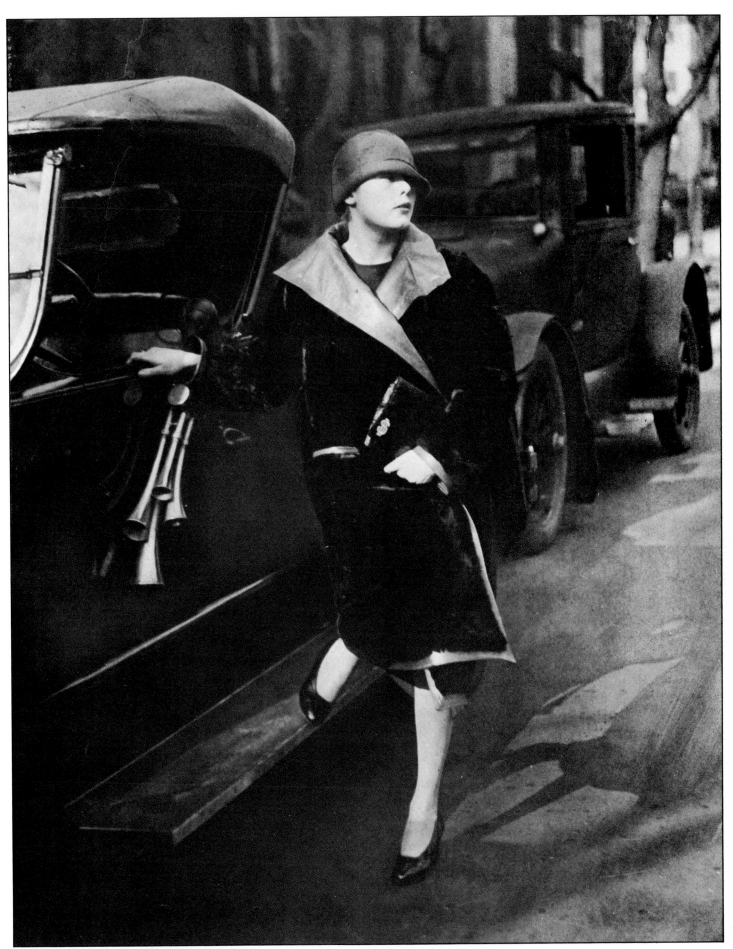

Poised and chic, the epitome of the sophisticated flapper, Suzette Dewey, daughter of the Assistant Secretary of the Treasury, steps out of her roadster.

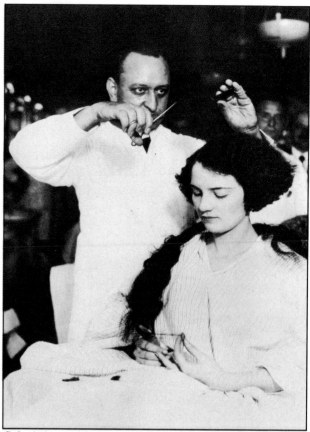

Submitting stoicly to a men's barber, a girl has her hair bobbed.

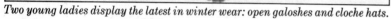

Two young ladies display the latest in winter wear: open galoshes and cloche hats.

An amateur artist decorates a flapper's full-length rain slicker.

Comic Joe E. Lewis displays patterned golf hose, baggy knickers and bow tie.

Patent-leather hair, center-parted, provides the movie-hero look.

A young man in Los Angeles proudly shows off his flappy white "Oxford bags."

Garbed in a raccoon coat and peekaboo hat, a lady of fashion enters her auto.

A girl in a short skirt and turned-down hose powders her knees.

Sporting snappy hats, saddle shoes and other insignia of youth, college-bound undergrads gather around a baggage truck for some close harmony.

High Life on the Campus

College was at the center of the upheaval that was shaking American manners and morals. The college man, with his ukulele and hip flask, was an irreverent but romantic figure who wore his hair combed back and stiffened with slickum; he thus fancied that he resembled the Hollywood idol, Rudolph Valentino, and he liked to be called a "sheik." His girl, or "sheba," pretended to be very liberated and delighted in raising the eyebrows of her elders. Said F. Scott Fitzgerald: "She would talk the language she had talked for many years—her line—made up of current expressions, bits of journalese and college slang strung together into an intrinsic whole, careless, faintly provocative, delicately sentimental." This slang formed almost a private language (Glossary, pages 280-281). "Hooch" and "giggle-water" meant liquor. "And how!" expressed emphatic agreement, as did "I should hope to tell you." A plain girl was a "jane," a beautiful one (or anything else desirable) was "the cat's meow." If, by chance, a sheba let loose at a fraternity party and started to dance on top of a table, the sheiks might cluster around her and shout, "Get hot!" If the girl wanted to get rid of a too persistent admirer, she might tell him scornfully, "Go fly a kite" or, perhaps, "Go cook a radish."

College students prided themselves on their cynicism. Most of them professed to have little interest in politics, and their rebelliousness seldom took the form of a desire to end social injustice or expose corruption in public office; they were too "disenchanted" (to use a popular word of the day).

There was a kind of ingenuousness in this self-conscious worldliness, and indeed in much of college life. The self-styled sophisticates of the campus were capable of the most naïve enthusiasms. Disdainful as they might pretend to be of social conventions, they were still eager to join a fraternity; the '20s saw the heyday of the "Greeks." Similarly, college kids turned out in droves for football rallies and games, and the captain of the football team was almost always the biggest man on campus.

To be sure, college wasn't all innocence; there had to be some fire underlying all that smoke. Anxious parents listened with horror to tales of student binges; some of the stories were certainly true. Many students had cars and used them to take dates to rowdy roadhouses and for "crashing" parties in distant cities. Party-crashing became a popular sport, and more than one dismayed hostess watched total strangers drink her liquor and pillage her house. After drunken weekends newspapers were filled with stories of automobile smash-ups.

College dances were sometimes wild affairs. Male students often brought chorus girls—or at least a few girls who were considered very "fast"; "hot numbers" were what was in fashion and not demure "nice" girls. Northern colleges had imported the cut-in dance from the South; twice as many men as girls might be invited, and the "stags" were expected to cut in on a couple several times during every number. If a girl had a good figure and a fast line of gab (preferably including a few off-color jokes), she was cut in on frequently; if not she often fled to the powder room to avoid the humiliation of dancing all evening with the same boy. This system encouraged flappers to dress and talk—and at least appear to behave—as wildly as possible.

Of course many colleges, particularly small rural institutions and those connected with religious denominations, maintained strict standards of student behavior. For example, dress regulations for girls at Northwest Nazarene College in Nampa, Idaho, specified: "Thin dress materials may be used provided suitable underslips are worn. Skirts must be of such length as not to expose the calf of the leg. Flesh colored or extremely thin hose are not permitted."

Nevertheless, such institutions were the exception. Campus after campus abolished compulsory chapel attendance, legalized smoking for women, did away with dress regulations and winked at drinking parties. On the subject of student immorality the nation was divided. While an official of the Y.M.C.A. was making the gloomy little prediction, "Pet and die young," the Pi Delta Literary Society at Queens College was listening to this debate: "Resolved. That it is easier to make love in a Ford than in a buggy."

Flaming Youth

Boxes and barrels stoke a Homecoming-eve bonfire at the University of Wisconsin.

Cornell freshmen stand ankle-deep in goo during mud-rush.

Fashionable University of Minnesota coeds sell chrysanthemums before a Homecoming football game in the early '20s, before short skirts were stylish.

Part of hazing, the spring mud-rush was dropped in 1926.

A flivver decorated with laundry proclaims its capacity: "40 men and eight horses."

A cheerleader stirs up enthusiasm at Louisiana State. At many schools participation in organized cheering was compulsory during sports events.

College Humor
THE BEST COMEDY IN AMERICA

We want to know if a sleeping bag is the same thing as a knapsack.

VASSAR VAGABOND

She doesn't drink,
She doesn't pet,
She hasn't been
To college yet.

TENNESSEE MUGWUMP

"Will your people be surprised when you graduate?"
"No, they've been expecting it for several years."

AMHERST LORD JEFF

"I'd love to have a leopard skin coat."
"Oh, my dear, they show spots terribly."

WISCONSIN OCTOPUS

"Will you have time to play a few pieces from Beethoven?"
"I'm sorry, miss, but this is my Bizet day."

M.I.T. VOO DOO

"Will you lend me five dollars for a month, old boy?"
"Listen, silly, what does a month-old boy want with five dollars?"

RICE OWL

First Poppa: Do you think your son will soon forget all he learned at college?
Second Poppa: I hope so; he can't make a living necking.

COLUMBIA JESTER

Theta: What's your brother like?
Beta: Wine, women and song.

WASHINGTON DIRGE

Marriage is an institution.
Marriage is love.
Love is blind.
Therefore marriage is an institution for the blind.

NEBRASKA AWGWAN

We call her Marigold because that's what she's trying to do.

GRINNELL MALTEASER

Then there was the modest old maid who wouldn't undress with the "Christian Observer" in the room.

SYRACUSE ORANGE PEEL

"I say, waiter, there's a fly in my soup!"
"Surely not, sir; maybe it's one of those vitamin bees you read so much about."

IOWA FRIVOL

Customer: Does this wig match my hair exactly?
Salesman: Yes, sir, like toupees in a pod.

OHIO GREEN GOAT

In order to create better feeling on the campus the co-eds have decided to discard their fur coats.

COLORADO DODO

Moronia thinks the postage stamp is a dance.
Well, letter.

STANFORD CHAPARRAL

Jokes, Campus Style (Groan!)

In 1923 a magazine was launched by a young man just one year out of college. His name was H.N. Swanson and the magazine was *College Humor*. Essentially the magazine offered little more than a digest of jokes and cartoons from campus humor publications. It was an instant success. Although it sold for 35 cents a copy—a high price for that time—it soon had 800,000 readers.

The comedy in most of the campus humor magazines, unfortunately, ranged from corny to dreadful. Bearing such strange names as *Mugwump, Ski-U-Mah, Awgwan* and *Malteaser*, the campus magazines concerned themselves mainly with necking parties, cutting classes, excessive drinking and outrageous puns. A certain amount of genuine wit, however, did sometimes glimmer feebly in *College Humor*, and H.L. Mencken even went so far as to say, "The contributions of freshmen are especially interesting. It takes a year or two of pedagogy to iron out a student of genuinely lively mind. By the time he is graduated he is usually ruined, but while he lasts he sometimes contributes something rich and racy to the national humor."

"I'm a mute."

"You don't say."

PENN STATE *FROTH*

"Busy?"

"No. You busy?"

"No."

"Then let's go to class."

COLGATE *BANTER*

"Jack's been jilted by a street cleaner's daughter."

"Why doesn't he sewer?"

PITT PANTHER

"I can tell you the score of the game before it starts."

"What is it?"

"Nothing to nothing—before it starts."

MINNESOTA *SKI-U-MAH*

Prof: Tell me the name of a German philosopher.

Victim: Can't, sir.

Prof: That's right.

NOTRE DAME *JUGGLER*

Co-ed: I'd like to look at some lynx fur.

Clerk: Lynx, lynx? I don't understand.

Co-ed: Oh, you must have them. This is a chain store, isn't it?

OKLAHOMA *WHIRLWIND*

"Whiskey kills more people than bullets."

"That's because bullets don't drink."

WASHINGTON AND LEE *MINK*

"Do you fellows wash your own clothes at the house?"

"Heck, no."

"Well, what's that washing machine for?"

"That's no washing machine. That's our cocktail shaker."

CORNELL *WIDOW*

She was so dumb she wondered how electric light poles grew in a straight line.

COLBY *WHITE MULE*

Prof: Can you give me an example of a paradox?

Plebe: A man walking a mile but only moving two feet.

ANNAPOLIS *LOG*

She may be an artist, but she seldom draws the line.

L.S.U. *PURPLE PEL*

"What's the man feeding the elephant moth balls for?"

"To keep the moths out of his trunk, silly."

IOWA *FRIVOL*

He may have been a ham, but his sugar cured him.

RUTGERS *CHANTICLEER*

She (demurely): Do you consider my legs long?

He: Yes, whenever possible.

V.P.I. *SKIPPER*

She: I want that car in the window.

He: Well, it's in the window.

VANDERBILT *MASQUERADER*

That Barbaric Music

"Social dancing," wrote a female evangelist in the Portland *Oregonian*, "is the first and easiest step toward hell. The modern dance cheapens womanhood. The first time a girl allows a man to swing her around the dance floor her instinct tells her she has lost something she should have treasured." What she usually lost was her corset. Most "nice" girls were forced by their mothers to wear foundation garments, but the flappers hated them; they discouraged men and made it uncomfortable to do dances like the black bottom, the shimmy and the Charleston. Therefore, as soon as girls arrived at parties they rushed into the ladies' room and "parked their girdles."

Once liberated, the girls were free to indulge in the slow fox trots of the day or to break loose during the faster, jazzier numbers. Jazz songs seemed somehow uncivilized—and therefore desirable—to the young. As one young man commented: "Our music is distinctly barbaric, our girls are distinctly *not* a mixture of arbutus and barbed-wire. After all, we have just discovered that we are still very near to the Stone Age." Whether savage or suggestive or just silly, the song lyrics captured the high spirits of the decade, as the excerpts below demonstrate.

Runnin' wild, lost control
Runnin' wild, mighty bold
Feelin' gay, reckless too.

I'm the sheik of Araby,
Your love belongs to me.
At night when you're asleep,
Into your tent I'll creep.

If you knew Susie like I know Susie,
Oh! Oh! Oh! what a girl!
We went riding, She didn't balk
Back from Yonkers,
*   I'm the one that had to walk!*

Doing the Charleston, three teams in St. Louis compete—with varying degrees of enthusiasm—in front of City Hall during a 1925 dance contest.

Restlessly pursuing thrills, Joan Crawford (wearing sequins in the car on the left) goes for a joy ride in her 1929 film, "Our Modern Maidens."

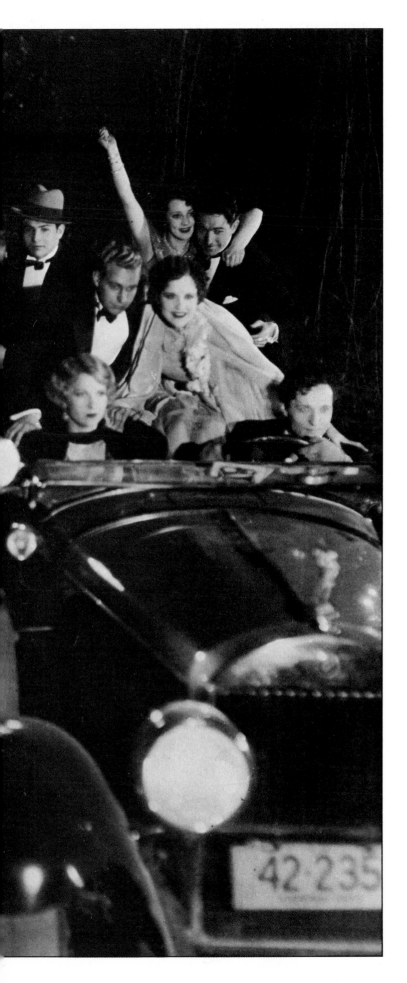

Hollywood Fans the Flames

In the '20s flaming youth learned to burn more brightly by imitating the antics of the stars in Hollywood movies. Girls copied the romantic techniques of great vamps like Theda Bara, studied sex appeal from Clara Bow *(next page)* and learned to smile winsomely from Mary Pickford.

One of the most popular screen flappers was Joan Crawford, who drew huge crowds in 1928 to her film about decadent youth, *Our Dancing Daughters.* Millions of girls watched breathlessly as Crawford drank, kissed and, best of all, showed how to cross and uncross one's hands on one's knees while doing the Charleston. The film was so

---

Joan Crawford is doubtless the best example of the flapper, the girl you see at smart night clubs, gowned to the apex of sophistication, toying iced glasses with a remote, faintly bitter expression, dancing deliciously, laughing a great deal, with wide, hurt eyes. Young things with a talent for living.

F. SCOTT FITZGERALD

---

successful that she made a sequel, *Our Modern Maidens.* In this one Crawford played a married woman who flirts with a bachelor, gets divorced and—scandalous!—lives happily ever after.

What Crawford did for the girls, Rudolph Valentino did for the boys. Following his lead, American men learned to tango, and to pop their eyes and bare their teeth while making love. Advertising copywriters did their part, too; one movie ad promised "brilliant men, beautiful jazz babies, champagne baths, midnight revels, petting parties in the purple dawn, all ending in one terrific smashing climax that makes you gasp." The films really were not quite that exciting, but they didn't have to be; they set off the nation's youngsters anyhow. "Those pictures with hot love-making in them," one 16-year-old girl told a writer, "they make girls and boys sitting together want to get up and walk out, go off somewhere, you know."

If there was any one person who made the kids get up and walk out it was Clara Bow, who turned the innocent little pronoun "It" into the most suggestive word in the language. Elinor Glyn, a popular author of love stories, had written a novel called *It*. In Madame Glyn's book, "It" was not a thing; it was a quality (always capitalized). She defined it this way: "To have 'It,' the fortunate possessor must have that strange magnetism which attracts both sexes. There must be physical attraction, but beauty is unnecessary."

When Madame Glyn came to Hollywood to find a girl who possessed "It," she elected Clara Bow, a tiny starlet with bee-stung lips, flat chest, big eyes and dimpled knees (the only other possessors of "It" that Madame Glyn found in Hollywood were all male: a Latin lover named Antonio Moreno, the doorman at the Ambassador Hotel and a stallion named Rex). Soon the "It" girl was one of the leading five box-office draws in Hollywood.

The story of her rise to stardom was like something invented by a press agent. She had been born very poor in Brooklyn. Scorned by other girls because of her shabby clothes, she turned to boys. When she was 16 she entered a beauty contest, won first prize and was whisked off to Hollywood for a bit part. Her performance ended up on the cutting-room floor, however, and her psychotic mother was so horrified at the prospect of her daughter becoming an actress that she tried to stab Clara. But the girl persevered, soon won recognition in several films and then, when she was 21, was dubbed the "It" girl.

Her off-screen life also made good copy. Living in a modest bungalow and dressing casually (she wore pants before most other women dared), Clara apparently drove men mad with desire. A Yale football player slashed his wrists after she jilted him; he survived to tell a court during a sanity hearing that Clara had kissed him so passionately on one occasion that his lips had been bruised for two days. She bathed in perfume and refused to hire a chauffeur because none would drive fast enough. By the end of the decade, her luck was running out. After the stock-market crash, people were bored by flappers; worse, the advent of talkies revealed that Clara had a thick Brooklyn accent. For a few brief years, however, Hollywood's "It" girl lived up to her billing as "The Hottest Jazz Baby in Films."

Clara Bow, languishing in a negligee, radiates "It," a quality she confusedly thought described the ability to give undivided attention in conversation.

F. Scott Fitzgerald studies one of his books. During the '20s he turned out three widely read novels; best known was "This Side of Paradise."

The Creator of an Era

Much of the credit—or the blame—for the flapper era must be laid on the shoulders of F. Scott Fitzgerald. An exceptionally handsome and talented young man, Fitzgerald became famous overnight in 1920 upon the publication of his first novel, *This Side of Paradise*. Fitzgerald was only 24, and he was one of the first writers to draw attention to the new postwar sophistication and to such phenomena as youthful love affairs and "petting parties." The book was a huge success and, in the words of a fellow writer, Fitzgerald became "a kind of king of our American youth." If he was king, the queen was his beautiful, witty and unstable wife, Zelda. The royal couple became almost as well known for their madcap antics as for his writing. They rode on the hoods of taxis down Fifth Avenue, disrupted plays by laughing during the sad parts and weeping noisily over the jokes, and entertained lavishly at drunken parties. To foot the bills for their extravagant capers, Fitzgerald wrote scores of short stories for the slick magazines; both the stories and his novels record—and partly served to create—the period. These are excerpts.

None of the Victorian mothers—and most of the mothers were Victorian—had any idea how casually their daughters were accustomed to be kissed. Amory saw girls doing things that even in his memory would have been impossible; eating three-o'clock, after-dance suppers in impossible cafés, talking of every side of life with an air half of earnestness, half of mockery, yet with a furtive excitement that Amory considered stood for a real moral let-down. But he never realized how widespread it was until he saw the cities between New York and Chicago as one vast juvenile intrigue.

THIS SIDE OF PARADISE

A moment later Muriel appeared in a state of elaborate undress and crept toward them. She was in her element: her ebony hair was slicked straight back on her head; her eyes were artificially darkened; she reeked of insistent perfume. She was got up to the best of her ability as a siren, more popularly a "vamp"—a picker up and thrower away of men, an unscrupulous and fundamentally unmoved toyer with affections.

THE BEAUTIFUL AND DAMNED

People over forty can seldom be permanently convinced of anything. At eighteen our convictions are hills from which we look; at forty-five they are caves in which we hide.

"BERNICE BOBS HER HAIR"

He (After due consideration): This is a frightful thing to ask.

She (Knowing what's coming): After five minutes.

He: But will you—kiss me? Or are you afraid?

She: I'm never afraid—but your reasons are so poor.

He: Rosalind, I really want to kiss you.

She: So do I. (They kiss—definitely and thoroughly.)

He (After a breathless second): Well, is your curiosity satisfied?

She: Is yours?

He: No, it's only aroused. (He looks it.)

She (Dreamily): I've kissed dozens of men. I suppose I'll kiss dozens more.

THIS SIDE OF PARADISE

The restlessness approached hysteria. The parties were bigger. The pace was faster, the shows were broader, the buildings were higher, the morals were looser, and the liquor was cheaper; but all these benefits did not really minister to much delight. Young people wore out early—they were hard and languid at twenty-one. Most of my friends drank too much—the more they were in tune to the times the more they drank. The city was bloated, glutted, stupid with cake and circuses, and a new expression 'Oh yeah?' summed up all the enthusiasm evoked by the announcement of the last super-skyscrapers.

COMMENTARY ON NEW YORK, 1926.

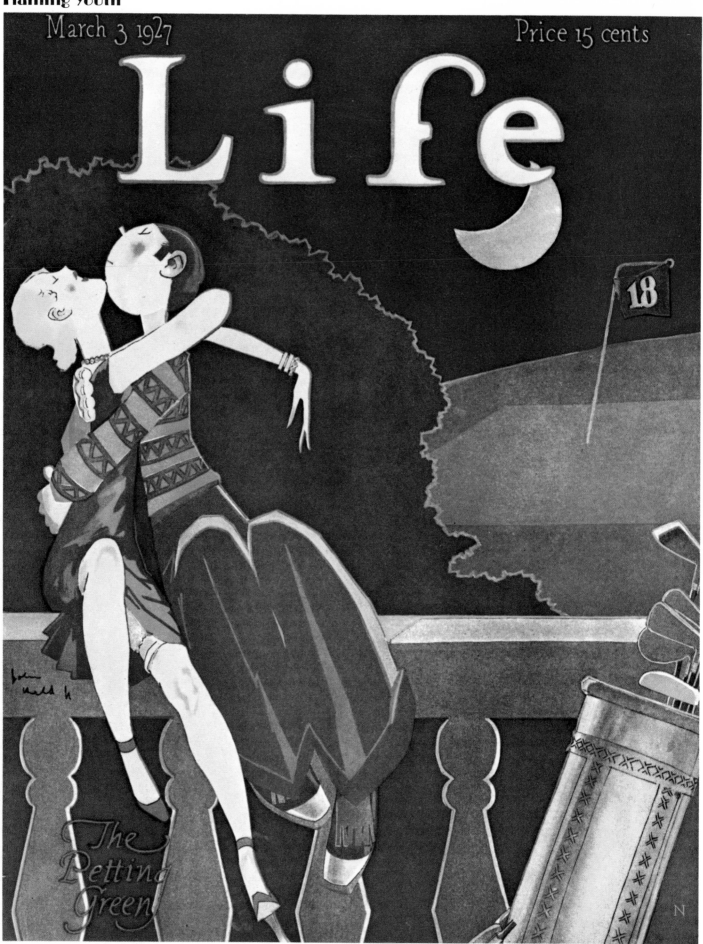

Life

The Petting Green

A button-nosed boy embraces a flapper on the cover of the humor magazine "Life." Held loved puns; this cover is entitled "The Petting Green."

Youth Sits for Its Portrait

The '20s have sometimes been called "The Era of Wonderful Nonsense." If F. Scott Fitzgerald wrote the dialogue for that era, John Held Jr., the decade's leading cartoonist, drew its portrait. On the covers of the old *Life* and *College Humor*, he developed the funny, stylish image of the flapper with her cigarette holder, shingle bob and turned-down hose and of her slick-haired boyfriend in puffy pants and raccoon coat. Soon it was hard to say whether Held was painting a true picture of youth or youth was aping his inventions.

Held was considerably older than the young collegiates he caricatured, and he never went to college. He was born in 1889 in Salt Lake City, where he worked on the high school newspaper with Harold Ross, the future editor of the *New Yorker*. He arrived in New York with exactly four dollars in his pocket and got a job in a newspaper art department. Soon his cartoons caught on, and he very quickly found himself earning a great deal of money. For one daily cartoon strip, *Margy*, he received $2,500 a week.

A rather eccentric man who raised horses, liked to tap dance in public and was covered with tattoos of eagles, anchors, girls and roses, Held once ran for Congress but refused to give any campaign speeches. He lost, and said he was relieved.

Actually, he took little time out to indulge in the frivolities he depicted. He was constantly at his drawing board. In 1928 he turned out, among other things, daily comic strips for the Hearst newspapers, wood engravings for the *New Yorker*, illustrations for various books (he had earlier illustrated Fitzgerald's *Tales of the Jazz Age)*, monthly frontispieces for *Red Book* and *Smart Set*, cartoons for *College Humor*, costumes and scenery for several theatrical productions, posters for the New Haven Railroad and dozens of small sculptures.

With all the money he earned, Held became a gentleman farmer on a large estate near Westport, Connecticut, where he kept a golf pro in residence and worked even harder, though he did occasionally take a break to tap dance for his Chinese chef, Chung Wi, or to dig ponds with the aid of his two mules, Abercrombie and Fitch. Although he loved to attend first nights of plays and was a member of several exclusive clubs, he was anything but the rowdy, curiously attired, gin-drinking sort of man he satirized. Perhaps his wry attitude toward the young people of the day was best summarized by the caption he supplied with a picture of a foolishly grinning, pipe-smoking, idiotically dressed boy in a floor-length raccoon coat: "One mother, one father, one tonsil-expert, four general practitioners, three trained nurses, five governesses, fifty-six ordinary teachers, thirty-two professors, and three athletic trainers combined their efforts to produce this."

John Held Jr. rests for a rare moment in the tweeds he always wore.

In cover illustrations artist John Held Jr. affectionately satirizes the flapper's dances, clothes and her new-found pleasure in driving a car.

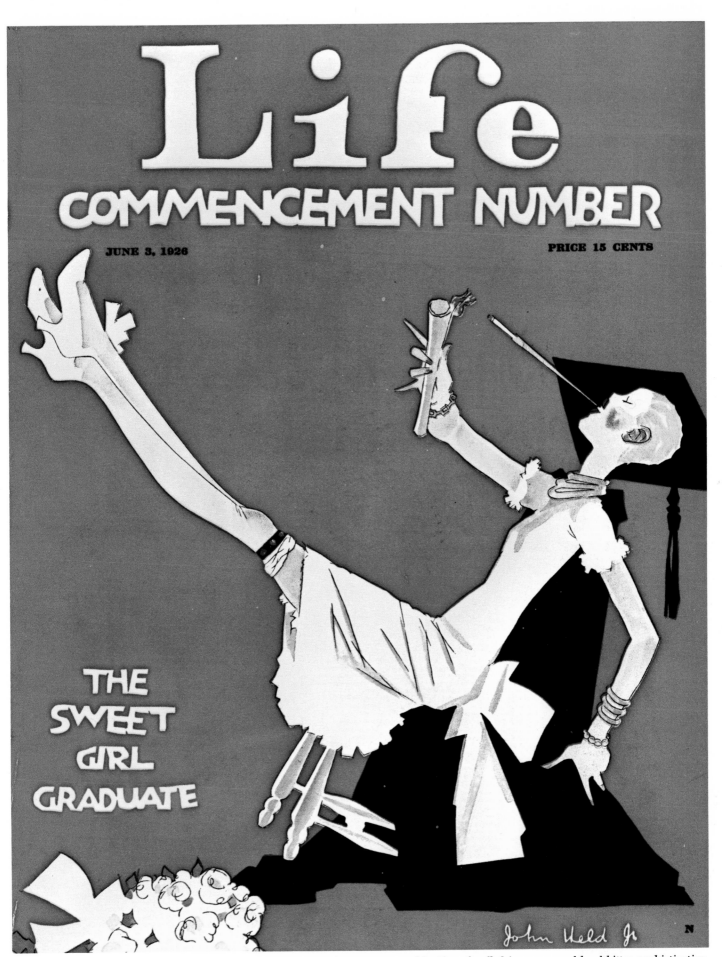

For the June 1926 number, Held pictures the modern coed as an incongruous combination of ruffled innocence and hard-bitten sophistication.

FROM A FRESHMAN'S LETTER HOME

"*Dear Mother:—Every morning I exercise with dumbbells.*"

"*Why so pensive, Spike?*"

"*I was thinking of a funny costume to wear at the masked ball.*"

THE USEFUL MISTLETOE

A VIEW OF THE BOAT-RACES

READY RELIEF... *The Girl Who Fainted at the Fraternity House Dance*

Flight

Massed bombers dedicate the new Hollywood airport in 1930.

A Suddenly Smaller World

The airplane has now advanced to the stage where the demands of commerce are sufficient to warrant the building of planes without regard to military usefulness. Undoubtedly in a few years the United States will be covered with a network of passenger, mail and express lines.

CHARLES A. LINDBERGH, *WE,* 1927

For American airmen, the early 1920s were years of frustration. During the war, many of them had known adulation; in particular, the folks back home had avidly followed the exploits of the pursuit pilots, whose man-to-man dogfights had supplied a touch of personal combat amid the mechanized slaughter of trench warfare. Now, most Americans had reverted to their old conviction that if God had wanted men to fly, He would have given them wings. Some fliers turned to other ways of making a living: Eddie Rickenbacker, America's Ace of Aces, sold autos. But there was a small group of men who doggedly stuck to the air; they soon found themselves engaged in a strange variety of airborne activities.

Ben O. Howard, pilot turned airplane designer, found a lucrative market in building planes for bootleggers, who needed the aircraft to smuggle illegal liquor across the Canadian or Mexican borders. Howard also flew the contraband cargoes himself—and got used to being shot at by moonshiners who thought they were being hunted from the air by revenue agents. Famed instructor and pilot Casey Jones sped urgent news photos cross-country. Another pilot, Roscoe Turner, set up an airline that ran from Los Angeles to Reno, renowned for quickie divorces; Turner's route became known as the "Alimony Special." After this venture folded, Turner convinced an oil company whose trademark was a lion that it could get enormous publicity if it hired him to fly around the country with a lion cub as his passenger. The lion liked to fly, but the Humane Society insisted that Turner strap a parachute on the beast. Luckily, the cub never had to jump.

That was more than could be said about the pilots who worked for the Post Office Department's infant air-mail service. Flying without instruments in all kinds of weather, many of them died when their planes iced up or hit mountainsides, but a good number were saved by their 'chutes. A tall, slender young air-mail pilot named Charles A. Lindbergh bailed out four times without ever losing faith in aviation. In 1927 Lindbergh took off from Roosevelt Field, Long Island, in a tiny plane, and headed out over the ocean, bound for Europe. Some 33.5 hours later he landed in Paris—and was stunned by the hysterical acclaim that greeted him. It was a justified tribute, for Lindbergh's exploit, the first nonstop solo transatlantic flight, was the transcendentally dramatic event which proved that the age of air transportation had truly begun. With this flight, the world was suddenly smaller.

Lindbergh stands beside "The Spirit of St. Louis." He identified himself with his plane so closely that he used the term "we" in telling of their flight.

Ormer Locklear, first to transfer from one moving plane to another, here adds a refinement by doing it head first. He later died in a filmed stunt crash.

Lillian Boyer, girl stunt flier, shows that her nerves are as good as any male's. Loops under the wings are to keep them from dragging during landing.

"Your Money Back..."

Moving across the country with the seasons, keeping their aging planes in the air with ingenuity and baling wire, landing in any level pasture, the barnstorming pilots of the 1920s gave at least 10 million Americans their first introduction to flying, at five dollars per five-minute joy ride. Most of them flew Jennies—war surplus JN-4D trainers, thousands of which had been completed too late for the war and could now be had for as little as $300 each.

To get customers out to the field, the barnstormers learned showmanship. At first they merely buzzed low over a town while stunt men walked out on the lower wing. Then, as competition grew stiffer, the stunters became more imaginative: they stood on the upper wing, dangled from the lower wing, parachuted to earth. A stunter would even drop from the plane without a chute, as onlookers gasped in horror; he fell freely for a few feet and then jerked to a stop at the end of a thin rope, invisible from the ground. Once when business was slow, stunt man Wesley May crouched on the top wing of a plane with a five-gallon can of gasoline strapped to his back, while another plane flew alongside, wingtip-to-wingtip.

Then May stepped across to the other plane, walked the length of its wing, and poured the fuel into its tank.

Aerial clowns were also good for business. "Wild Bill" Kopia's act was a favorite. Dressed as a bosomy operatic soprano, he would buy a ticket and climb into the passenger cockpit of a Jenny whose propeller was idly ticking over. Suddenly the pilot would jump out, presumably to get something he'd forgotten, and at that moment the Jenny would lurch forward with the apparently terrified "soprano" yelling for help. Nearing the boundary fence, the Jenny would abruptly climb into the air and then Wild Bill would put on a superb demonstration of aerobatics, to the delight and astonishment of the crowd.

The financial returns for taking these risks were skimpy. Dick Depew, one of the barnstormers, once remarked solemnly that "the most dangerous thing about flying is the risk of starving to death." It was certainly true that barnstorming was safer than it looked, for the pilots were among the most skilled airmen of their time. "All rides are guaranteed to get you back in one piece," one pitchman used to cry. "Your money back if you get killed!"

Airborne tennis at 70 mph was one of the wilder crowd-pleasing stunts. Unseen by nervous spectators were cables holding the players to the wing.

A mail pilot, bundled up, prepares to board his Boeing. This plane had a passenger compartment; travelers no longer had to hold the mail on their laps.

Carrying the Mail

Scheduled air mail had an inauspicious beginning. On the very first flight, a Washington-New York run, the plane started to take off, then stopped; someone had forgotten to fill the fuel tank. The mail finally got off the ground, but the pilot became lost and made a forced landing in Maryland. The flight never did get to New York.

In the years that followed, the mail got through with increasing regularity, but only because the pilots were extraordinarily capable and heedless of danger. Planes had no radio and few navigational instruments; weather forecasts were issued "without assuming any responsibility for accuracy." Thirty-one of the first 40 pilots to fly the mail from New York to Chicago were killed in crashes.

In spite of the odds, the fliers took pride in getting the mail through, and on time. Congressional appropriations were scarcely more dependable than the weather forecasts, and the airmen knew that money to keep the mail aloft depended on their performance. On February 22, 1921, pilot Jack Knight landed in Omaha after a 248-mile flight from North Platte, Nebraska, one leg of a history-making trip—the first transcontinental day-and-night delivery (previously the planes had landed at nightfall). Knight was looking forward to a long sleep when the field manager informed him that no pilot was available for the next leg, a 424-mile jaunt to Chicago.

Uppermost in the minds of both men was the knowledge that Congress would be voting next day on the mail appropriation. Knight climbed back into the plane and took off on the unfamiliar route. He arrived at his refueling stop, Iowa City, in heavy snow, then flew through thick fog to a triumphant landing in Chicago. All together he had been aloft in his open plane for 10 grueling hours. Two other pilots completed the journey to New York; total elapsed time across the continent had been 33 hours 20 minutes—an incredible record for the period. Congress passed the bill. Soon better planes came into service, and air-postage rates, reflecting the growing dependability of the mail, dropped from 24 cents to 10 cents a half ounce. A stamp was issued showing the rate change (above)—a signal to mail pilots that the service had finally come of age.

AIR   RAIL   AIR   RAIL

COAST TO COAST IN 48 HOURS

(Daily Through service effective from New York July 7—from Port Columbus July 8, 1929)

The schedule and meal arrangements for the through route between New York, N. Y. and Los Angeles, Cal., and San Francisco, Cal., are given below. Passengers will be ticketed from Pittsburgh, Cleveland or any station on the Pennsylvania Railroad on convenient connecting train service to and from Columbus. Tickets will be also sold from all stations for any combination of rail and air service included in the through route.

WESTBOUND

Pennsylvania Railroad
THE AIRWAY LIMITED
Eastern Time
Lv. New York (Penna. Sta.),
  N. Y.*............ 6.05 PM
Lv. North Philadelphia, Pa. 7.50 PM
Lv. Washington, D. C.... 6.30 PM
Lv. Baltimore, Md....... 7.30 PM
Ar. Port Columbus, O.†... 7.55 AM

Transcont'l Air Transp. Inc.
Lv. Port Columbus, O.... 8.15 AM
        Central Time
Ar. Indianapolis, Ind...... 9.13 AM
Lv. Indianapolis, Ind...... 9.28 AM
Ar. St. Louis, Mo........12.03 PM
Lv. St. Louis, Mo.‡.....12.18 PM
Ar. Kansas City, Mo...... 2.47 PM
Lv. Kansas City, Mo...... 3.02 PM
Ar. Wichita, Kansas...... 4.56 PM
Lv. Wichita, Kansas...... 5.11 PM
Ar. Airport, Okla. (Landing
  Field)§............ 6.24 PM
Transfer to Waynoka by Aero Car

Atch., Topeka & Santa Fe Ry.
*Sleeping car ready for occupancy
at 8.00 PM*
        Central Time
Lv. Waynoka, Okla......11.00 PM
Ar. Clovis, N. M.‖....... 8.20 AM
Transfer to Portair by Aero Car

Transcont'l Air Transp. Inc.
        Mountain Time
Lv. Portair, N. M. Landing
  Field.............. 8.10 AM
Ar. Albuquerque, N. M...10.17 AM
Lv. Albuquerque, N. M...10.32 AM
Ar. Winslow, Ariz........ 1.12 PM
Lv. Winslow, Ariz.‡...... 1.27 PM
        Pacific Time
Ar. Kingman, Ariz........ 2.31 PM
Lv. Kingman, Ariz....... 2.46 PM
Ar. Los Angeles, Cal..... 5.52 PM
(Grand Central Air Terminal, Glendale, Cal. Passengers will be transferred by Aero Car to and from the central section of Los Angeles.)

EASTBOUND

Transcont'l Air Transp. Inc.
        Pacific Time
Lv. Los Angeles, Cal. 8.45 AM
  (Grand Central Air Terminal,
  Glendale)
Ar. Kingman, Ariz.......11.18 AM
Lv. Kingman, Ariz.‡.....11.33 AM
        Mountain Time
Ar. Winslow, Ariz....... 2.14 PM
Lv. Winslow, Ariz....... 2.29 PM
Ar. Albuquerque, N. M.** 4.40 PM
Lv. Albuquerque, N. M.... 5.10 PM
Ar. Portair, N. M. Landing
  Field.............. 6.54 PM
Transfer to Clovis by Aero Car

Atch., Topeka & Santa Fe Ry.
*Sleeping car ready for occupancy
at 9.00 PM*
        Central Time
Lv. Clovis, N. M........11.35 PM
Ar. Waynoka, Okla.⊙.... 8.10 AM
Transfer to Airport by Aero Car

Transcont'l Air Transp. Inc.
        Central Time
Lv. Airport, Okla. Landing
  Field............... 8.55 AM
Ar. Wichita, Kansas...... 9.55 AM
Lv. Wichita, Kansas......10.10 AM
Ar. Kansas City, Mo......11.43 AM
Lv. Kansas City, Mo.‡....11.58 AM
Ar. St. Louis, Mo........ 2.00 PM
Lv. St. Louis, Mo........ 2.15 PM
Ar. Indianapolis, Ind...... 4.22 PM
Lv. Indianapolis, Ind...... 4.37 PM
        Eastern Time
Ar. Port Columbus, O.... 7.15 PM

Pennsylvania Railroad
THE AMERICAN
Lv. Port Columbus, O.*... 7.46 PM
Ar. North Philadelphia, Pa. 8.05 AM
Ar. New York (Penna. Sta.),
  N. Y.............. 9.50 AM
Ar. Baltimore, Md........ 9.05 AM
Ar. Washington, D. C.....10.05 AM

San Francisco passengers upon arrival at Los Angeles will be given the option of using overnight trains either from Los Angeles or Glendale, or they may remain overnight in Los Angeles and proceed by Maddux Airline plane morning service from Glendale Airport to San Francisco. Transfers will be provided by aero car between Glendale and the central section of Los Angeles. Tickets for whichever plan is selected by passenger will be furnished by the Transcontinental Air Transport, Inc.

From San Francisco passengers will be given the option of using overnight trains from San Francisco, arriving Glendale next morning, making direct connection with eastbound airplane, or they may leave San Francisco via Maddux Airline afternoon plane, arriving Grand Central Air Terminal, Glendale and will be transported by Aero car to the central section of Los Angeles. The next morning they will be transported by Aero car to the airport at Glendale.

*Dinner and breakfast on Pennsylvania Railroad Dining Car. †A new station stop (Port Columbus) seven (7) miles east of Columbus, O. ‡Luncheon on plane—Fred Harvey Service. §Transfer to Harvey House, Waynoka, Okla., where dinner will be served. ‖Breakfast at Harvey House, Santa Fe Station—**Dinner at Albuquerque, Airport—Fred Harvey Service. ⊙Breakfast at Harvey House

Apply to any Pennsylvania Railroad agent for full information as to fares, checking baggage, other schedules, etc.

PENNSYLVANIA RAILROAD

This announcement of combined air-rail service in 1929 promised travelers a 36-hour saving over the fastest train. Dark blocks indicate night travel.

Profits from Passengers

After Lindbergh's flight to Paris, Americans took to the skies in increasing numbers. Watching air passenger figures quadruple in 1928, financiers decided that aviation might actually prove profitable. Securities were marketed, the infant airlines ordered big trimotor airplanes, and new airports were built to accommodate them.

But night travel was still considered too hazardous for passenger operations. The first coast-to-coast service was set up as a hybrid: the travelers flew by day, transferred to train at night; the entire trip took a solid, exhausting two days. The service was launched with enormous fanfare. The maiden journey departed from Los Angeles on July 8, 1929; eastbound, Lindbergh himself piloted the plane, which had been christened by screen star Mary Pickford. Enthusiasm for air travel was running high, but it was far from universal. The president of one airline admitted that he never flew in his company's planes when he could avoid it—and his wife flatly refused to fly at all.

Passengers board the Fokker with which Pan American began its international service in 1928. One-way fare, Key West to Havana, was $50.

Travelers buy air tickets at a counter in the Cleveland Automobile Club.

This prototype of air terminal buildings was at Ford Airport, Detroit.

If a passenger and his baggage topped 180 pounds, he had to pay extra.

This Ford Tri-motor boasted a steward and weightsaving wicker seats.

The ample costumes of the first stewardesses combated cabin drafts.

Snappily uniformed pilots are briefed in the latest navigation methods.

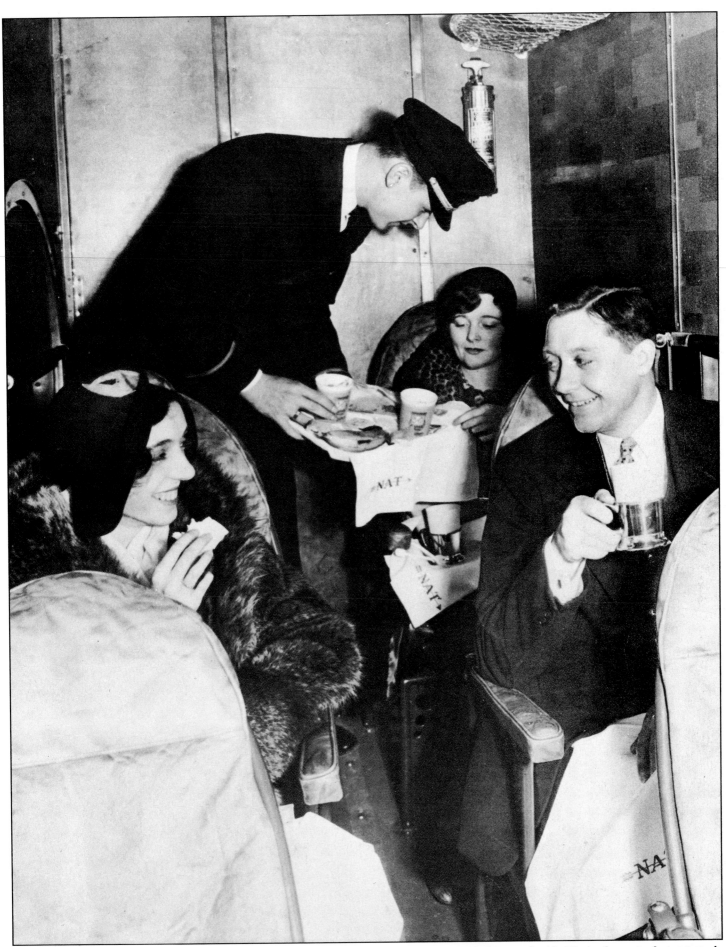

A steward serves up a meal. At one point airlines used weighty crockery, designed to stay put in bumpy air. Airsick travelers got a lemon to suck.

Airline publicity photos stressed the luxury features of the new transport planes, such as this Fokker F-32 sleeping compartment with tapestried panels.

Flight

Stout Air Lines, owned by Ford, was the first airline to carry mail, but was hampered by Henry Ford's refusal to open his Detroit airport on Sunday.

All That Jazz

Living Rooms in the Air

Though more and more people were flying, the vast majority of Americans continued to view air travel with dark suspicion. To counteract the resistance of the you'll-never-get-me-up-in-one-of-those-things set, airlines and plane-makers launched a great promotion campaign. The Ford Motor Company—which in the '20s made not only autos but airplanes and also operated its own airline—ran advertisements extolling the virtues of commercial flying. "Those who hesitate to employ the airplane," one ad admonished sharply, "will do well to recall that there are still many old-timers who refuse to ride in automobiles!"

Decorators were called upon to design cabin interiors that resembled living rooms. But the psychological effect was spoiled by the difficulty of talking above the engine noise and the occasionally disconcerting leap of a cup of coffee as the plane hit an "air pocket." To prepare passengers for these little surprises, Ford's Stout Air Lines issued a booklet from which the excerpts below are taken.

Don't worry. Relax, settle back and enjoy life. If there's any worrying to be done, let the pilot do it; that's what he's hired for. Be patient while the plane taxis to the corner of the field before taking-off. The luxury of flying doesn't appear until you begin to use the third dimension.

The pilot always banks the plane when turning in the air. Take the turns naturally with the plane. Don't try to hold the lower wing up with the muscles of the abdomen—it's unfair to yourself and an unjust criticism of your pilot.

The atmosphere supports the plane just as firmly as the ocean supports a ship. At the speed you are traveling, the air has a density practically equivalent to water; to satisfy yourself, put your hand out the window and feel the tremendous pressure—your guarantee of absolute safety.

The wind is similar to an ocean current. At flying levels it is usually as regular as a great, smooth-flowing river. Once in a while the wind is gusty and rough. These gusts used to be called "air-pockets" but they are nothing more than billows of warm and cool air and nothing to be alarmed over.

Dizziness is unknown in airplanes. There is no discomfort in looking downwards while flying because there is no connection with the earth; only a sense of confidence and security, similar perhaps, to what birds feel. Owing to the altitude, you may think you are moving very slowly, although the normal flying speed of the Stout-Ford plane is 95 miles an hour.

When about to land the pilot throttles the engine, preparatory to gliding down to the Airport. The plane can be landed perfectly with the engine entirely cut off. Under no occasion attempt to open the cabin door until the plane has come to a full stop.

The Stout-Ford all-metal plane is the safest in the world. Built by the great Ford organization, made entirely of duralumin metal and steel alloys, it is the strongest plane of its type in the world. It is automatically stable. Were the pilot to put it in any position and then release the controls, it would return automatically to the normal flying position.

Our motto is: Safety—First, Last and Always. In addition to employing only the safest plane, we maintain a daily inspection far more rigorous than any ever given to any other form of vehicle. Your pilot is one of the best in the country. An expert motor and plane mechanic flies every trip and is also trained as an alternate pilot. Nothing is omitted that we believe may add to your safety and comfort. Hence we repeat—settle back, or move around as you wish, enjoy the trip, and—Get the Maximum Enjoyment out of your Flight!

The Company is not liable for any damages by reason of damage or injury to any passenger or to his goods or baggage.

Stout Air Lines, owned by Ford, was the first airline to carry mail, but was hampered by Henry Ford's refusal to open his Detroit airport on Sunday.

All That Jazz

Carroll Dickerson's band plays for a jazz floor show: Chicago, 1924.

The Syncopated Sound

Aw, play that thing, Mr. St. Cyr, lawd, you know you can do it! Everybody from New Orleans can really do that thing!

LOUIS ARMSTRONG TO THE BANJOIST ON "GUT BUCKET BLUES"

This was the Jazz Age. The word took the country, or at least the country's youth, by storm. Dressmaking establishments advertised "jazz styles," poets wrote "jazz poetry." *The New York Times* reported in 1925 that Fifth Avenue matrons were vying hotly for Negro maids who could teach them how to do the Charleston.

Of course this behavior, and the music that prompted it, scandalized the guardians of the nation's morals. An upstate New York preacher fulminated: "Jazz may be analyzed as a combination of nervousness, lawlessness, primitive and savage animalism and lasciviousness." A Columbia University professor of music denounced it as the attempt of "a joyless industrial civilization to arouse its fatigue-poisoned minds and its drudgery-jaded bodies."

These cries of anathema affected the rage for jazz to about the same extent that Prohibition kept people from drinking. And jazz lovers soon had impressive reinforcements. Serious composers quickly grasped at elements in the new syncopated music. Darius Milhaud, a leading French modernist, wrote a ballet with jazz rhythms; Paul Hindemith weighed in with jazz piano suites; Maurice Ravel published a sonata with jazzy passages. America's great song writer George Gershwin produced "serious" jazz compositions. These works sent the classical music critics into fits. Lawrence Gilman scathingly described Gershwin's *Rhapsody in Blue* as "trite," "feeble," "vapid," "fussy" and "futile."

But this "symphonic jazz" and most of the other music that passed for jazz in the '20s was not real jazz at all. The real music—like much great art through the centuries—was being produced in relative obscurity. It had moved upriver from New Orleans, its birthplace, but it was still heard mainly in Negro dance halls in Harlem and Chicago, and on records that were frankly labeled "race records" and sold only in Negro neighborhoods. And while the impresarios of ersatz jazz such as Paul Whiteman were making a quarter of a million dollars a year, the real jazzmen were often broke. The great Louis Armstrong had to play in dubious show bands such as Carroll Dickerson's *(pages 76-77),* while Bix Beiderbecke wasted his glorious cornet tone tooting for third-rate dance bands. The real jazzmen traveled from date to date in rattletrap cars with the luggage tied on the roof. But the musicians were tough and so was the music and it survived the neglect of the age to which it gave the name and became America's one triumphant contribution to the world's music.

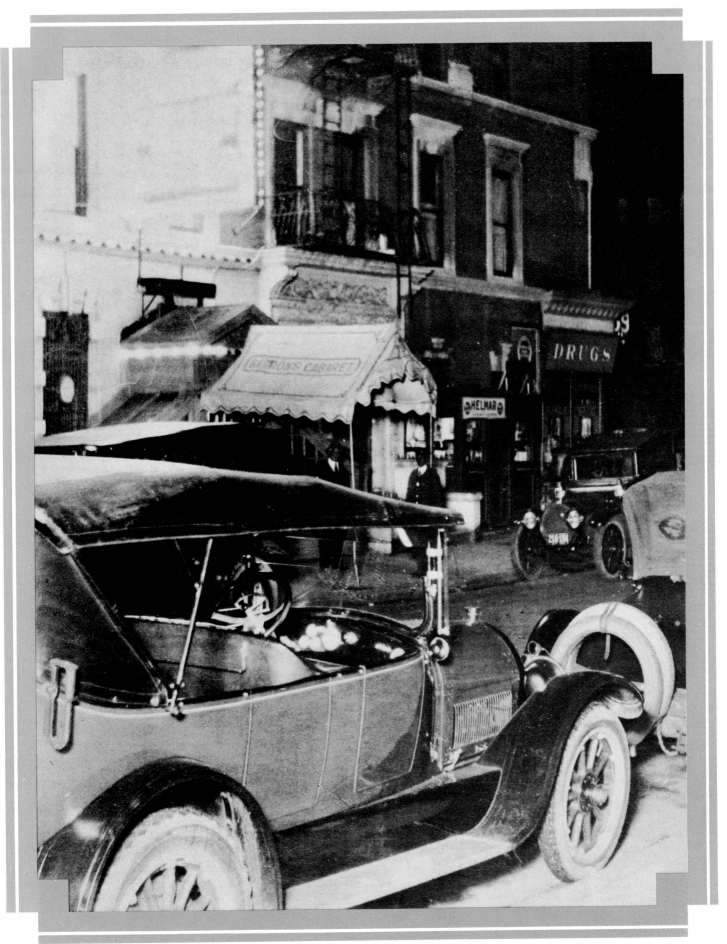

A modest canopy advertises Barron's Cabaret, a Harlem joint where jazz flourished. Duke Ellington got his start here in 1923.

In clownish poses, de rigueur for early jazz photos, King Oliver's Creole Jazz Band seems ready to blast the ears off pianist Lil Hardin.

DAGUERRE
Chicago

The King's Men

Who played the real stuff? The Negroes of Chicago's South Side agreed that the best group of all in 1923 was King Oliver's Creole Jazz Band. The name "Creole" indicated its origin—the band was almost a Who's Who of the best musicians to come north from New Orleans. Johnny Dodds played the clarinet and his younger brother, called "Baby," was on drums. Joe Oliver, the cornet-playing leader, had long been acknowledged the Crescent City's top brass man and he had with him a new cornet-playing sensation from down home, a cheerful lad named Louis Armstrong. Joe and Louis could read each other's mind and when they did duet breaks, playing in perfect harmony with no rehearsal, the crowd at Chicago's Lincoln Gardens went wild, standing on tables and shouting. The band had, everyone agreed, "that great blue New Orleans sound," and Joe Oliver deserved his title of King.

Oliver was a powerfully built man of formidable girth. When he was about to blow something really hot he would say to the admirers grouped around the bandstand, "Now you'll get a chance to see Papa Joe's red underwear." And as he blew chorus after chorus his stiff shirtfront would pop and the red undershirt—he always wore one—would show through. "I never blew my horn over Joe Oliver at no time," Armstrong recalled, "unless he said, 'Take it!' Never. Papa Joe was a creator—always some little idea —and he exercised them beautifully. I'll never run out of ideas. All I have to do is think about Joe."

A great man, a great horn, a great band. The South Side of Chicago was something else. The Lincoln Gardens, as one patron remembered, was "dingy and needing several coats of paint. Ancient paper decorations and faded flowers hung dejectedly from unpainted walls and peeling columns." Like other South Side joints, it received visits from the toughest kind of gangsters—members of Al Capone's mob. When fights or shooting erupted, it was the band's job to play as loudly as it could to cover up the noise of shattering bottles or gunfire. The musicians themselves often carried pistols. But despite the sordid surroundings and the violence, this is where true jazz first found an increasing audience and its own real voice.

Feather, fringe and a bright smile: Bessie Smith in 1925.

The Empress and Father Dip

A press agent made up the name "Empress of the Blues," but that is what Bessie Smith truly was. She sang with a power and an intensity of feeling unmatched by any other blues singer. Her records sold in the millions—although only in the South and the ghettos of the North. Her sound, as poet Langston Hughes said, "was too basic for the general public" and few white people in the '20s even knew her name. The records brought her a great deal of money. Unfortunately she spent it as fast as it came in. "A cat came up to her one day, wanted change for a thousand dollar bill—trying to see if she had it," Louis Armstrong recalled. "Bessie said, 'Yeah.' She just raised up the front of her dress and there was a carpenter's apron and she just pulled that change out of it. That was her bank."

The other towering figure in jazz as the '20s progressed was, of course, Armstrong himself—considered by many to have been, in his prime, the greatest jazz musician of them all. Born on July 4, 1900, he grew up in the toughest

Aw blow that thing, Father Dip! Umm, umm, that certainly is good!
KID ORY TO ARMSTRONG ON "GUT BUCKET BLUES"

black neighborhood in New Orleans. At 12 he was put in a home for wayward boys for firing off a pistol on New Year's Eve. It was there, in the reformatory, that he learned the rudiments of playing the cornet. Released from the home, he hawked coal from a mule-drawn cart, delivered milk, worked on a junk wagon and stevedored on the docks. At night he took jobs playing his battered horn in rough cafés; during this period his principal income came from the tips prostitutes gave him to play the blues. It was a hard school, but Armstrong was good enough by 1920 to get jobs on Mississippi River excursion steamboats and, in 1922, to join Joe Oliver in Chicago. Before long he was overshadowing even the great King Oliver and, like Bessie, was famous in the Negro world. His great soaring solos and his magnificent trumpet tone remade jazz. As a boy, his large mouth and lips had given him the taunting nickname of Dippermouth. Now his fellow musicians, in awe and affection, gave him another nickname—Father Dip.

Louis Armstrong in the mid-'20s: boiled shirt, shy grin and gleaming trumpet, the brilliantly toned horn he had exchanged for the cornet.

That Harlem Hotcha!

Suddenly Harlem was the thing. Its shows, as *Variety* proclaimed, had "pep, pulchritude, punch and presentation." And white people from downtown flocked northward to see them, especially the elaborate revues at Connie's Inn and the Cotton Club, both nightclubs catering mainly to white customers. Other clubs, of course, welcomed Harlem's own people and one dance hall, the Savoy, and one theater, the Lafayette, became hubs of night life.

The rage to visit Harlem and see Negro entertainment was triggered in 1921 when a superb musical show called *Shuffle Along*—written, produced and performed by Negroes—was a smash hit on Broadway. It was followed within a four-year period by eight other Negro shows including *Liza, Runnin' Wild* and *Chocolate Dandies*. Broadway playgoers had never known music like this, or seen such dancing or heard such singing. They wanted more, and the big Harlem clubs obliged with chorus lines, comedians, singers like Ethel Waters and marvelous dancers like Bill "Bojangles" Robinson. The clubs also provided the best big jazz bands of the period, notably Duke Ellington's and Fletcher Henderson's. But the bands were not, by and large, what the white folks went to see. They wanted, as *Variety* condescendingly put it, "high yaller gals" who could "uncork the meanest kind of cootching." They were, in effect, slumming and out for new thrills.

Few could appreciate the music any more than they could see the real Harlem. But they were at least exposed to jazz, and their dollars helped it flourish. Harlem in the '20s developed no fewer than 11 nightspots *Variety* called "class white-trade night clubs," plus some 500 other jazz places. "The swarming, prosperous crowds bent on nocturnal diversion," as one observer put it, "found Harlem exotic and colorful. To them it seemed a citadel of jazz and laughter where gaiety began after midnight."

Underneath the glitter, of course, all was not gaiety. This was, after all, Prohibition, and the owners of the Cotton Club included such unsavory bootleggers and gunmen as Owney Madden and George "Big Frenchy" De Mange. "Pineapples," as the people of the '20s called bombs, sometimes flew through the front windows of cabarets and blew out the back walls. But despite the violence, despite the segregation in the "class white-trade" places, despite the bad booze in the speak-easies, the idiom of Harlem crossed the continent and the oceans.

The influence of jazz, good and bad, began to spread. Its dissemination was aided by the phonograph record: dozens of companies vied to get on wax the newly famous Negro stars, along with their white imitators. Almost unnoticed amid all the cooch dancers and chorus lines, the great music was making its mark on the nation.

Colored singing and playing artists are riding to fame and fortune with the current popular demand for "blues" disk recordings and because of the recognized fact that only a Negro can do justice to the native indigo ditties such artists are in great demand.

VARIETY, JULY 26, 1923

Connie's, on Seventh Avenue at 132nd Street, is the first white outpost on the uptown colored frontier, the first stop on the route of the downtown night clubbers. Walk down one flight of stairs and you are in this rendezvous, so low-ceilinged as to be cave-like. Around the dance floor is a three-foot barrier built in the semblance of a village, miniature bungalows and villas, and here and there a spired church, through the tiny windows of which comes the gleam of midget lights. If these lights in the windows remind any of the customers of home, sweet home they certainly show no outward signs of such tender thoughts in Connie's. You can tell Connie's is a high class joint as soon as you sit down, because the waiter usually whispers that bottles should be carried in the pocket, and not be placed on the floor.

NEW YORK *DAILY NEWS*, NOVEMBER 1, 1929

To render a "Blues" song effectively, it is necessary to play the role of the oppressed or depressed, injecting into his or her rendition a spirit of hopeful prayer. "Blues" are more naturally blue when the melodic movements are treated with minor chords. It is possible to properly produce "Blues" effects on any instrument, although the wailings, moanings, and croonings, it can be understood, are more easily produced on instruments like the saxophone, trombone, or violin. Without the necessary moan, croon or slur, no blues number is properly sung.

"HOW TO PLAY AND SING THE BLUES LIKE THE PHONOGRAPH AND STAGE ARTISTS," A BOOKLET BY PIANIST PORTER GRAINGER AND ARRANGER BOB RICKETTS, 1926

Harlem has attained pre-eminence in the past few years as an amusement center. From midnight until after dawn it is a seething cauldron of Nubian mirth and hilarity. One sees as many limousines from Park and upper Fifth Avenue parked outside its sizzling cafes, "speaks," nightclubs and spiritual seances as in any other high-grade white locale in the country.

VARIETY, OCTOBER 16, 1929

What's jazz, lady? If you don't know, I can't tell you.

FATS WALLER TO A WHITE VISITOR TO HARLEM

Maude Russell leads her "Ten Ebony Steppers" through a lively number in "Just a Minute," one of many Negro shows that played Broadway.

Colorful labels marked products of companies that rushed to record the new music—as performed by both Negro artists and white imitators.

An elegant George Gershwin puffs a cigar and makes musical notations in a 1927 portrait by the great photographer Edward Steichen.

Matchless Melodies and "Symphonic" Jazz

Perhaps the most celebrated musical event of the decade was the premier of George Gershwin's *Rhapsody in Blue* at Manhattan's Aeolian Hall in the winter of 1924. Many of New York's bluest blue bloods and all of its music critics practically stormed the old concert hall. Paul Whiteman, the chubby bandleader who conducted the *Rhapsody*, went out front before the concert started and saw a mob scene. "Men and women were fighting to get into the door," Whiteman reported, "pulling and mauling each other as they sometimes do at a baseball game, or a prize fight, or in the subway." The furor outlasted the concert; the critics either praised the music or damned it unmercifully. Deems Taylor, considered the dean of the critics, was for it. He found that the *Rhapsody* revealed "a genuine melodic gift and a piquant and individual harmonic sense." Taylor added, "Moreover, it is genuine jazz music."

It wasn't at all, of course—"symphonic jazz" perhaps, but not the real article. Nevertheless, though Gershwin didn't write jazz, he was the beau ideal of the Jazz Age. He was handsome, forceful, independent and charming —and he became quite rich. Above all he was spectacularly successful in an era that worshipped success. It was not quite rags to riches, although people often said it was. His parents were Russian immigrants, but Morris Gershovitz—that was the real family name—always had enough money for food, and even piano lessons. Nevertheless George had moved from a boyhood on the Lower East Side to the best salons of New York and London, where he hobnobbed with millionaires, duchesses and other celebrities of the time. And he was an undoubted genius at writing the show tunes that everybody whistled and hummed. Not just show tunes but whole shows full of them. And marvelous ones. They were original, fresh, clever, timely, and often quite beautiful—"Lady Be Good," "I've Got a Crush on You," "The Man I Love," "Someone to Watch Over Me," "Looking for a Boy" . . . the list could go on and on.

These tunes were not jazz (jazz was a way of performing music, rather than a way of writing it); but, ironically, many quickly became "jazz standards"—that is, tunes jazzmen loved to play and improvise around. Another irony of Gershwin's relationship with jazz is that he himself adored the music. As a boy of eight he would roller skate through Harlem to 134th Street and sit on the curb outside Barron D. Wilkins' club and listen to that proto-jazz called ragtime float out the door. The first song on which he collaborated with his lyric-writing brother Ira proclaimed that "the great American folk song is a rag." His own piano playing had a very jazzy touch—angular, swift, offbeat. But he couldn't write the stuff, as the bemused critics and public thought. He was just a great song writer, possibly the best that ever lived.

If Americans adored George Gershwin, they went absolutely (and inexplicably) mad for Paul Whiteman and his orchestra. A young violinist from Denver, Colorado, Whiteman came East in 1920 and was soon acclaimed the King of Jazz—or sometimes the Prince, as in this ditty published in *Vanity Fair*:

> *J is for JAZZ by our plump Prince of Whales*
> *Whiteman, who staggers the musical scales.*

By 1922 he could command $25,000 for a six-night engagement, an enormous sum at the time and one that was unmatched for decades. When he married a dancer named Vanda Hoff it was front-page news. When he went on a diet and managed to lose 100 pounds—normally his face and figure resembled comedian Oliver Hardy's—two books were written about his ordeal. When he went to Europe he was so lavishly entertained that he gained 40 pounds back. On his return he was honored with a reception at the Waldorf-Astoria. The reason for this adulation is hard to imagine. Whiteman frequently had a topflight musician or two in his band (Bix Beiderbecke was one who played for him), but otherwise it was a mediocre outfit that burbled along without much beat, tone or imagination. Its popularity was, in short, a fad, an aberration of the dizzy decade. But there was nothing ephemeral about the real jazz, the glorious crazy-quilt of sound that spilled out of Barron Wilkins' and a thousand other joints to add the spice of originality to American music.

Sincerely Paul Whiteman

Paul Whiteman, baton in his hand, conducts the so-called jazz orchestra, strings and all, that galvanized the dancers of the '20s.

Panic roils Wall Street on October 24, 1929.

Boom and Bust

Business Fever

We have had booms and collapses in the past. But now we have no boom. Our progress is rapid—but sure. Buying is now larger than it ever was—but it is not frenzied. The kind of emotion which brings on a boom is absent.

SAMUEL CROWTHER IN *COLLIER'S*, 1926

When President Coolidge declared in 1925 that "The business of America is business," he was putting it mildly—and belatedly. Three full years had passed since the end of the postwar recession, and business had become a national obsession. Everyone was spending avidly and the economy was spiraling upward at a record clip.

Production was up. The torrential output of consumer goods included such desirable new products as radios and electric refrigerators, along with countless improved models of standard items—faster cars, shinier bathroom fixtures, even plusher caskets. Competition for sales was healthily stiff—and getting stiffer all the time.

Corporate profits were up. Thanks to new techniques of mass production, many manufacturers netted huge sums that they liberally plowed back into plant expansion. In 1923 U.S. Steel was operating so efficiently that it was able to reduce its workday from twelve to eight hours, to employ 17,000 additional workers, to raise wages and yet, amazingly, to show an increase in profits.

Income was up in most lines of endeavor. Even the industrial workers, whose strikes for higher pay had availed them little in the previous decade, benefited from company largesse and enjoyed a higher standard of living. To round out the happy picture, prices were stable; savings and life insurance doubled; and business was given added impetus by the growth of chain stores and installment buying. With all these factors reinforcing the upward spiral, prosperity seemed to have no ceiling.

In the full flush of fiscal euphoria, the country brought its swollen profits and abundant credit to bear in wild get-rich-quick speculation. By 1928 the prices of stocks had soared beyond the point of safe return as thousands of "little" people braved the hectic market seeking a share in overnight windfalls. A nurse made $30,000, a broker's valet amassed the tidy sum of a quarter-million.

At no time in the '20s were more than 1.5 million Americans involved in the market, but their much publicized successes fueled the reckless optimism of the country at large. Business, most people came to believe, would provide everyone with a steadily increasing share of ever-expanding prosperity. It now seemed almost unpatriotic to exercise restraint in buying. It seemed heretical to pay any heed to the likes of economist Roger Babson, when he warned: "Sooner or later a crash is coming, and it may be terrific." America was a nation of giddy consumers for whom wishful thinking had become a way of life.

A 1921 cartoon entitled *"The Anglers"* shows shady operators fishing for victims in the stock exchange—a graphic warning widely ignored.

Living-Room Credit Purchases

PIANO—$445	LARGE RUG—$148.50	SOFA—$74.50	CORNER CABINET—$37.95
$15 down, $12 a month	$10 down, $15 a month	$5 down, $8 a month	$5 down, $5 a month

Other Household Items   VACUUM CLEANER—$28.95   REFRIGERATOR—$87.50   WASHING MACHINE—$97.50

$2 down, $4 a month $5 down, $10 a month $5 down, $8 a month

EASY CHAIR—$38.50
$5 down, $5 a month

PHONOGRAPH—$43.50
$5 down, $5 a month

BEDROOM SUITE—$228.00
$15 down, $15 a month

Those Easy Little Payments

"Pay as you ride," invited the auto-makers. "Enjoy while you pay," cajoled the appliance manufacturers. And the consumer, responding with enthusiasm, bought more and more of industry's goods on some sort of deferred payment plan. Between 1920 and 1929, installment purchases quintupled, reaching six billion dollars annually. Time purchases in 1929 accounted for 90 per cent of all piano, sewing- and washing-machine sales, over 80 per cent of vacuum cleaner, radio and refrigerator sales, 70 per cent of furniture sales, and 60 per cent of auto sales.

For people everywhere, easy credit opened up broad new vistas. One study showed that in Muncie, Indiana, working men who earned $35 a week often spent $35 a month paying for the family car. In Chicago, investigators found one man who earned $60 a week but was shelling out $27.50 of it for home furnishings and his wife's coat. The question was—how much credit buying could the individual and the country stand? Opinion divided sharply. Gloomy predictions were voiced by traditionalists who counted it a virtue to live within one's means. An Oregon banker, well aware that installment buying added between 11 and 40 per cent to the cost of an article, took a strong position against "mortgaging future earnings for the gratification of present-day pleasures."

On the other hand, newfangled economists considered credit buying a healthy handmaiden of prosperity. One such optimist, writing in *Collier's* weekly, suggested that the phrase, "Smith has large debts," was not really damning but complimentary, for it meant that "Smith has a fine line of credit."

On some points, however, almost all the disputants agreed. First, the "easy little payments" were a confounded nuisance; and second, they were an excellent topic for casual humor. A whole series of sardonic two-liners went the rounds. In one such joke the husband says, "One more payment, and the furniture is ours," to which his wife replies, "Good. Then we can throw it out and get some new stuff." Another joke had the husband saying, "I just paid the doctor another ten dollars on his bill." The wife's reply: "Oh goody, two more payments and the baby's ours."

99

Joining the radio craze, a shopper listens through earphones. The number of radio-owning families was 60,000 in 1922 and 13,750,000 in 1930.

The Radio Business

Of all the new products put on the market during the decade, none met with more spectacular success than the radio. As late as 1919, the radio audience was a scattering of avid hobbyists listening over earphones to barely audible crystal sets. Yet in the new decade radio quickly became a big business—twice over, in fact, as hardware for home entertainment and as a medium for advertising.

Radio had its practical beginning in 1920, when station KDKA in Pittsburgh announced the returns of the Harding-Cox Presidential election. Inspired by this modest triumph, KDKA began the first regularly scheduled broadcasting of news, church services and music. By the end of the decade, 618 stations were in business, and networks were regularly broadcasting from coast to coast.

The increasing availability of free home entertainment created a soaring demand for radios. Large-scale manufacturing operations began in 1920. Radio sales rose from less than two million dollars that year to $600 million in 1929.

At first, the airwaves were considered a public trust that must be kept unpolluted by commercialism. Even a trade journal for advertisers declared, "Any attempt to make the radio an advertising medium would, we think, prove positively offensive to great numbers of people." But that was in 1922, and in the same year the first sponsored program was broadcast over station WEAF in New York. The advertiser, a real-estate corporation, was discreet enough, merely announcing itself as the sponsor without breathing a word in praise of its house lots. But this innocent precedent opened the floodgates.

The losing battle against commercial sponsorship was joined by Dr. Lee De Forest, whose invention of the three-element vacuum tube had helped make big-time radio possible. Long after radio programs *(overleaf)* had become firmly identified with sponsors' products, De Forest was still inveighing against advertising. "What have you done with my child? You have sent him out on the street in rags of ragtime to collect money from all and sundry. You have made of him a laughingstock of intelligence, surely a stench in the nostrils of the gods of the ionosphere."

Billy Jones and Ernie Hare were sponsored by Happiness Candy.

The Clicquot Club Eskimos were led by Harry Reser, standing with banjo;

Jessica Dragonette sang, and Ford Bond announced, for Cities Service.

Some Programs and Their Sponsors

SUNDAY, OCTOBER 6, 1929

5:30 (p.m.)—WEAF—Philco Hour:
Philadelphia Orchestra.
Leopold Stokowski conducting.

8:00—WJZ—Enna Jettick melodies.

8:30—WEAF—Chase & Sanborn
Choral Orchestra: Phil Ohman and
Victor Arden, piano duo.

9:15—WEAF—Atwater Kent
Orchestra: Hazel Arth, contralto;
Ted Roy, tenor.

11:00—WJZ—Amos 'n' Andy.

MONDAY, OCTOBER 7, 1929

7:30—WJZ—Roxy and His Gang.

8:00—WEAF—Firestone Orchestra:
Franklyn Baur, tenor;
Vaughn de Leath, contralto.

8:30—WEAF—A & P Gypsies
Orchestra.

9:30—WEAF—General Motors Family

Party: Sousa's Band.

9:30—WJZ—Chesebrough
Real Folks, sketch.

TUESDAY, OCTOBER 8, 1929

7:30—WEAF—Soconyland Sketch:
Rhode Island's Blow for Liberty.

8:00—WJZ—Pure Oil Band.

9:00—WEAF—Eveready Symphony
Orchestra: Mario Chamlee, tenor.

9:00—WJZ—Johnson and Johnson,
musical melodrama.

9:00—WABC—Old Gold:
Paul Whiteman Orchestra.

9:30—WJZ—Dutch Masters Minstrels.

10:00—WEAF—Clicquot Eskimos'
Orchestra.

10:30—WEAF—RKO Hour: Reisman's
Orchestra; Morton Downey, tenor.

WEDNESDAY, OCTOBER 9, 1929

7:30—WOR—Kellogg Radio Town

The sponsor's ginger ale was praised by announcer Graham McNamee (right).

Rudy Vallee and Graham McNamee were on for Fleischmann's Yeast.

Crier: Alexander Woollcott;
Otis Skinner.

8:30—WEAF—Wonder Bakers
Orchestra: Jack Parker, tenor.

9:00—WEAF—Ingram Shavers
Orchestra.

10:30—WJZ—Stromberg-Carlson
Orchestra: Clyde Morse, piano.

THURSDAY, OCTOBER 10, 1929

8:30—WJZ—Champion Sparkers
Orchestra: sports drama.

9:30—WEAF—Jack Frost's
Melody Moments.

9:30—WJZ—Maxwell House
Orchestra.

10:00—WEAF—Halsey, Stuart
Orchestra: talk,
"The Old Counselor."

10:30—WEAF—Victor Orchestra:
Gloria Swanson, screen star.

FRIDAY, OCTOBER 11, 1929

6:30—WEAF—Raybestos Twins: Al
Bernard and Billy Beard;
Lannie Ross, tenor.

7:00—WJZ—Mallory Hatters
Orchestra.

SATURDAY, OCTOBER 12, 1929

8:30—WEAF—Laundryland Lyrics:
Bernice Taylor, soprano;
Fred Waldner, tenor.

9:00—WEAF—General Electric
Symphony Orchestra,
Walter Damrosch conducting.

9:30—WJZ—Gillette Orchestra.

10:00—WEAF—Lucky Strike
Orchestra.

10:00—WABC—Paramount Orchestra:
Moran and Mack; Anne Boughman,
soprano; Veronica Wiggins,
contralto; quartet.

Goodrich's Masked Tenor turned out to be little-known Joe White.

Boom and Bust

1920—1,111 stores   WOOLWORTH   1929—1,825 stores

1920—4,621 stores   A & P   1929—15,418 stores

1920—312 stores   J.C. PENNEY   1929—1,395 stores

1920—12 stations   STANDARD OIL OF NEW JERSEY   1929—1,000 stations

1927—1,681 stores   FIRST NATIONAL STORES   1929—2,002 stores

1926—766 stores   SAFEWAY STORES   1929—2,660 stores

1920—3 stores   WESTERN AUTO SUPPLY CO.   1929—54 stores

1920—6 stores   LERNER SHOPS   1929—133 stores

1920—1,243 stores   AMERICAN STORES   1929—2,644 stores

1920—515 stores   PIGGLY WIGGLY   1929—2,500 stores

1920—184 stores   S. S. KRESGE   1929—597 stores

1921—2,000 stores   UNITED CIGAR STORES   1929—3,700 stores

Lengthening Chains

The average housewife of the '20s knew little about the merchandising revolution that was spreading networks of chain stores from coast to coast. But she had a keen appreciation of the advantages offered by fast-growing chains (left) in many fields. Canned pears from Bohack's, a lunch of pancakes at Childs, aspirin from a United Drug store, a summer frock from Lerner's, an oil change at an Esso station and Fanny Farmer mints—all such chain items had some special attraction, be it lower price, wider selection, greater reliability, better service or simply convenience and familiarity.

For the housewife and the chain alike, economy was the ruling passion. Chains cut costs through volume purchasing and heightened efficiency, and passed on a part of the saving to the consumer. The gigantic A & P chain, which bought a half-billion dozen eggs a year, could afford to set its price per dozen several cents lower than that of the small-scale independent grocery—the so-called "Ma and Pa" operation. Comparable cost-price benefits stemmed from a different source at the F.W. Woolworth Company. Its 1,500 five-and-ten-cent stores were stocked with rewarding economy by only 36 expert buyers.

Salary savings were even more important to a trail-blazing company in the fiercely competitive grocery business, which was crowded with 860 rival chains by 1928. This particular firm, Piggly Wiggly, featured a method of operation new to the field at the start of the decade. Under the proud slogan "Scientific Merchandising," Piggly Wiggly created a self-service system, with its markets laid out according to a patented traffic pattern. The stores —the first supermarkets—were popularly known as grocerterias until the handier term was coined.

The self-service format worked spectacularly well. Piggly Wiggly boasted the nation's highest average sales per customer. Reflecting and insuring its success were prices that undercut larger chains with greater purchasing power. In 1921 Piggly Wiggly offered three pounds of a national-brand coffee for $1.05, while a conventional service store charged $1.55. Even A & P, the biggest egg merchant of them all, could not match the Piggly Wiggly price of 36 cents a dozen. If thrift was demanded by a housewife's budget, she scrambled eggs purveyed by Piggly Wiggly.

For all the battles fought between chains and independents, decisive victories were few and far between, but a resounding triumph was won in the movie-theater field, and it revamped the young industry. In earlier, harder times for the trade, film producers licensed their movies for exhibition through distributors to theater owners; the three parties were, for the most part, separate interests. But as movies became more popular, costly and profitable, a natural trend toward consolidation swiftly developed. By 1922 average weekly theater admissions totaled 40 million, and the figure doubled in the next seven years. This business—at ticket prices never less than 10 cents and often more than 75 cents at first-run theaters—was very big business, well worth fighting for.

The movie makers, being the source of the lucrative product, started with the upper hand, and were able to

Loew's Paradise, a victim of Bronx zoning, lacked the usual marquee.

rig their policies so as to overwhelm and take over many distributors. The big producers also bought up theaters, as much to shut out their rivals' films as to make more money exhibiting their own. In the dog-eat-dog struggle to assemble big chains, one of the sharpest sets of teeth belonged to the brilliant head of Paramount, Adolph Zukor, whose goal was nothing short of a complete monopoly. Using stealthy mergers and brute cash freely, Zukor snapped up theaters singly and in whole chains, and acquired small producers to boot. More and more theaters fell into fewer and fewer hands. By 1927 the field was practically denuded of important independents. The nation's 20,000 theaters, along with some 600 distributors, had been forged into a few long chains owned or controlled by great producers.

During and after the war for existing outlets, new theaters were built at a frantic rate, and these, like the theater chains, got bigger and richer steadily. The movie palaces of the '20s were just that, palaces—edifices as huge and lavish as the celluloid dreams they offered. The really big theaters, such as the Roxy in New York and the Fox in Detroit, seated some 5,000 people. New York's Capitol Theater, seating 5,300, was so cavernous that a movie magazine remarked, "The mezzanine floor looks as if it had been designed for eight-day bicycle races."

Everything in these deluxe palaces was on a commensurate, inflated scale. Vast and opulent accommodations overawed the customer: imperial staircases, kingly rest rooms, princely chambers for depositing children in an attendant's care. Gilded ornaments, sumptuous rugs, marble statuary, ponderous crystal chandeliers, epic murals, and ceilings painted with fleecy clouds—these and other sensations were laid on with a trowel. Every style of architecture and decoration known to man was used in one theater or another, and sometimes many of them could be discerned in a single theater. Indeed the taste for flamboyance was dignified by stylistic names hitherto unknown: the San Francisco Fox *(opposite)*, one of several palaces decorated by Fox's wife Eve Leo, was said to be an outstanding example of "Early Eve Leo."

The spectacular lobby of the San Francisco Fox had its own pipe organ, atop the grand staircase, to regale moviegoers awaiting the next show.

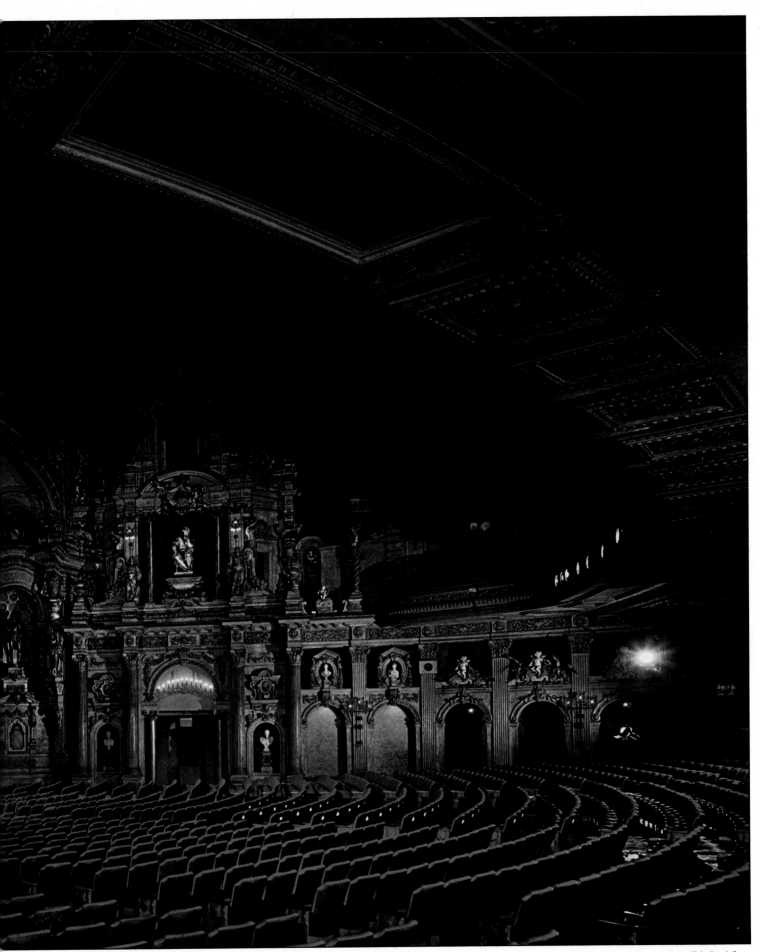

In Loew's Paradise, 3,936 customers could enjoy the movie in comfort amid a veritable museum of Renaissance-like statuary in gilded niches.

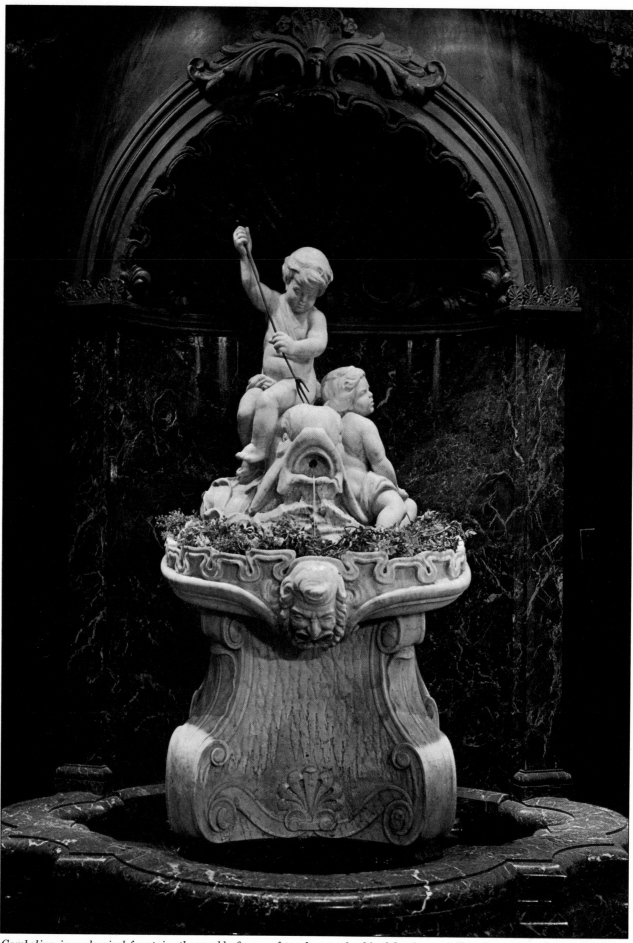

Gamboling in a classical fountain, the marble figures of two boys and a big fish adorn a lobby alcove in the Loew's Paradise.

An $80,000 work of art, this exotic organ was custom-made by Wurlitzer for Detroit's Fisher Theater and lavishly decorated with Mayan motifs.

Prosperous and confident, members of the Minneapolis Commercial Club assemble for a working lunch, to boost local business and civic projects.

The Benevolent Boosters

Business in the '20s was a cult with legions of high priests. These were the boosters—thousands of businessmen who belonged to Rotary, the Kiwanis, the Chamber of Commerce, the Lions, the Elks. These organizations conspired diligently to advance the interests of local business. They proclaimed the community's virtues, encouraging new businesses to open there. They sought ways to protect local businessmen from the inroads of the national chain stores and mail-order companies; their posters urged everyone to "Patronize your NABORHOOD stores."

To their credit, the boosters usually entertained loftier purposes than mere gain. All worked for charitable causes and for such organizations as the Boy Scouts. The Lions backed a campaign to provide the blind with white canes; Rotary sought, "through an interchange of thoughts and experiences and activities, to educate its members."

Predictably, the boosters were often satirized for their backslapping camaraderie, their unsophisticated zeal, their unquestioning conformity to old-fashioned ideals. Naturally, too, such robust men easily weathered the barbs of H. L. Mencken and Sinclair Lewis. More remarkably, they also survived their own propaganda, including a prayer for businessmen that included the following lines.

*God of business men, I thank Thee for the fellowship
    of red-blooded men with songs in their
    hearts and handclasps that are sincere;
I thank Thee for telephones and telegrams that link
    me with home and office, no matter where I am.
I thank Thee for the joy of battle in the business
    arena, the thrill of victory and the courage to
    take defeat like a good sport;
I thank Thee for children, friendships, books, fishing,
    the game of golf, my pipe, and the open
    fire on a chilly evening.*   AMEN

A dedicated salesman, advertising executive Bruce Barton preached and practiced sincerity in his trade, writing copy that rang with evangelic zeal.

The Supersalesman

To the business community of the '20s, salesmanship was the greatest of the performing arts. And the greatest of the salesmen were those who dedicated themselves to what Sinclair Lewis facetiously called "the cosmic purpose of Selling—not of selling anything in particular, for or to anybody in particular, but pure Selling."

Such supersalesmen turned up in many guises (overleaf). But no one fitted the description better than Bruce Barton (left), who sold everything imaginable, with profligate brilliance. The son of a poor Tennessee preacher, he sold newspapers to put himself through Amherst College. Then he sold his talents to wartime acquaintances and with them founded the advertising firm of Batten, Barton, Durstine & Osborn. A copywriter par excellence, in his ads he sold collars, safety razors, literary classics.

Then in 1924, Barton scaled new heights of salesmanship. To provide a little uplift, he dashed off *The Man Nobody Knows*, which became a bestseller. The book, excerpted below, put forth the startling thesis that the title character—Jesus—was the world's greatest salesman.

Surely no one will consider us lacking in reverence if we say that every one of the "principles of modern salesmanship" on which business men so much pride themselves, are brilliantly exemplified in Jesus' talk and work. The first of these and perhaps the most important is the necessity for "putting yourself in step with your prospect." Instantly he won his audiences. With his very first sentence he put himself in step with them; it was invariably a thought in line with their own thinking, easy for even the dullest to understand, and shrewdly calculated to awaken an appetite for more.

He would be a national advertiser today, I am sure, as he was the great advertiser of his own day. Take any one of the parables, no matter which—you will find that it exemplifies all the principles on which advertising text books are written.

1. First of all they are marvelously condensed, as all good advertising must be. Jesus hated prosy dullness.

2. His language was marvelously simple—a second great essential. All the greatest things in human life are one-syllable things—love, joy, hope, home, child, wife, trust, faith, God.

3. Sincerity glistened like sunshine through every sentence he uttered. The advertisements which persuade people to act are written by men who have an abiding respect for the intelligence of their readers, and a deep sincerity regarding the merits of the goods they have to sell.

4. Finally he knew the necessity for repetition and practiced it. No important truth can be impressed upon the minds of any large number of people by being said only once.

Jesus had a wonderful power to pick men, and to recognize hidden capacities in them. What a list of disciples! Not a single well-known person on it. Nobody who had ever made a success of anything. A haphazard collection of fishermen and smalltown business men, and one tax collector—a member of the most hated element in the community. What a crowd!

He thought of his life as business. What did he mean by business? To what extent are the principles by which he conducted his business applicable to ours? Manufacturers; presidents of railroads and steamship companies; the heads of banks and investment houses—all tell the same story. "Service is what we are here for," they exclaim. They call it the "spirit of modern business"; they suppose, most of them, that it is something very new. But Jesus preached it more than nineteen hundred years ago.

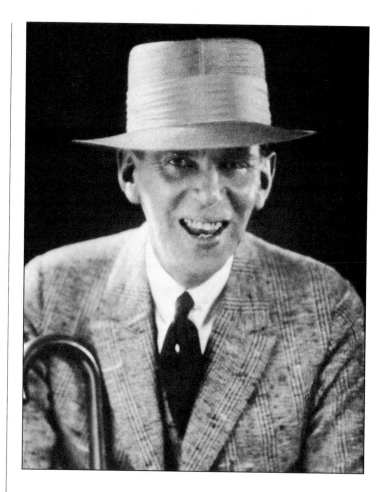

A Master Swindler

To the vocation of swindling, Charles Ponzi brought the quintessence of salesmanship: a manner that inspired confidence. Starting out in Boston, he used his charms to mount a ludicrous scheme. Claiming that he made huge sums by sending a type of postal money order from country to country to take advantage of favorable exchange rates, Ponzi accepted deposits and signed unsecured notes promising to repay the principal plus 50 per cent in 90 days. Ponzi paid off scrupulously; soon he had opened branches in 28 Northeastern cities. But in August 1920, reporters learned that Ponzi had served a term for forgery in Montreal; subsequent investigations disclosed he had only $1.6 million to show for $15 million in funds received. Ponzi was sent to prison and was ultimately deported.

But many Bostonians, including his victims, remembered him with undiminished affection. Their loyalty was perhaps captured best by a story in *The Boston Post*, which told of a crowd that formed to encourage Ponzi after the law caught up with him. "You are the greatest Italian of them all," cried one fervent supporter. Ponzi modestly demurred, nominating instead Columbus and Marconi, and explaining that they had discovered America and radio. "But," another person protested, "you discovered money."

The Prince of Promoters

A promoter and publicist with talents to match his size (six feet four inches and 250 pounds), Wilson Mizner made millions selling people almost everything, and in a haphazard career that took him from the Guatemalan jungles to the Klondike gold fields, he dignified each exploit with at least one memorable witticism. One of his projects was managing the boxer Stanley Ketchel; and when Mizner was told that the great middleweight had been killed in a quarrel, he replied incredulously, "Start counting ten over him. He'll get up at nine." He sold his gifts as a playwright to Hollywood, whose attraction for him was a reputation for glamorous immorality; "I thought," he informed his countless friends, "that it would be like taking a ride through a sewer in a glass-bottom boat."

Mizner's greatest promotion was staged in Florida. When a land boom started there in 1924, he and his brother Addison went into the hotel and land development business. The two did so well that Wilson was offered $1.3 million for his interests. He turned down the deal and ended up broke when the boom fizzled. For this reverse, too, Mizner had an apt epigram: "Always be pleasant to the people you meet on the way up, because they are always the very same people you meet on the way down."

Wizard of the Utilities

In later, sadder times for Samuel Insull, the Chicago-based public utilities magnate was haunted by unproved charges of shady corporative manipulations, whose exact nature was too complex for his prosecutors to describe comprehensively, much less to understand fully. But in the permissive '20s, his main offense lay in exploiting with unprecedented success certain legal loopholes that he often urged legislators to close. For self-protection more than gain, Insull created a vast pyramid of nonworking trusts and holding companies, then mass-marketed stocks in those firms and used the proceeds to secure his hold on dozens of working companies worth billions.

At the peak of his power around 1929, Insull was nationally renowned as both a financial wizard and a paragon of civic virtue—a sort of beneficent Midas. Applying many technological improvements in the utilities field, and pioneering others himself, he lowered electric rates appreciably, which won him public gratitude and political immunity. Indeed he was held in such awe that bankers often phoned him to offer loans. According to Insull's bookkeeper, the lords of finance said in effect, "We have some nice fresh green money today, Mr. Insull. Isn't there something you could use maybe ten million dollars for?"

A Genius at Slogans

Because his father was president of the American Tobacco Company, George Washington Hill succeeded him in that post in 1926. But Hill, a ruthless man with a gift for selling, had already proved his ability to handle the job. In his first coup, he had produced for the company's Lucky Strike cigarettes a multi-million-dollar slogan: "It's toasted." This claim was a reference to the heating treatment by which Luckies processed tobacco; Hill, undeterred by the fact that all cigarette makers used heat processing, based a huge advertising campaign on the notion that toasting removed harmful impurities but not the flavor. Hill followed up this slogan with an even more successful one. In 1926, when Lucky Strike ranked third to Camel and Chesterfield, Hill made a daring appeal to diet-conscious women: "Reach for a Lucky Instead of a Sweet." This campaign made Luckies the best-selling cigarette.

For these and other triumphs, Hill was hated and feared. For his legendary displays of vulgar showmanship (such as framing Luckies packs in the windows of his Rolls-Royces, and spitting on a desk for special emphasis), Hill was ridiculed, abused and called "a particular pain in the neck." But the supreme indignity was understatement; Hill once was described as a "dramatic personality."

The Golden Dawn of Total Advertising

Lionized and romanticized, the advertising men of the '20s were prone to forget how far their vocation had come since the turn of the century. In that dim recent past, advertising's function remained primarily and politely informative—to announce and describe a product interestingly, lest potential customers fail to buy out of abysmal ignorance. Most advertising was so restrained that one job-hunting copywriter got himself hired by uttering what then seemed to be a startlingly new and aggressive definition: "Advertising Is Salesmanship in Print!"

In that go-getter spirit, the soft sell hardened as competition increased apace with the volume and variety of manufactured goods. Concurrently, the mass-marketing revolution broke down the lingering vestiges of regional merchandising, making it possible to advertise national brands in national magazines—this with the newly added impact of full-color printing. Thus the great postwar boom ushered in the age of all-out advertising. By 1925 the magazines and newspapers owed 70 per cent of their total income of $1.3 billion to ad revenue.

Under the tempering heat of competition, the modern advertising agency emerged in the '20s as a sophisticated team of high-paid specialists. Ad agencies earned their commissions by doing far more than creating and placing ads; their various experts often named, packaged, priced and promoted the distribution of the product. Great ad men could, and did, bestow instant success on fledgling products and sick businesses. Albert Lasker, the brilliant owner of the Lord & Thomas agency, was largely responsible in 1920 for selling America a rather shopworn firm and its untested new product—the Republican party and Warren G. Harding. And the rewards for success were fabulous. Lord & Thomas' resident genius, Claude C. Hopkins, who was widely regarded as the first and greatest of the great copywriters, took home as much as $300,000 in annual salary and commissions.

Marking the ads of the '20s were several traits that they shared with the decade itself, such as brashness and a lack of scruples. Many ads trafficked in quasi-factual, pseudo-scientific details: a mouthwash boasted the approval of exactly 45,512 doctors, none of them named, and a shaving cream stated with weighty significance that it expanded 250 times upon contact with water. Another phenomenon was the popularity of testimonial ads, which brought fees of up to $5,000 to celebrities in every field. Composer George Gershwin, actress Constance Talmadge and a heroic steamship captain all declared, in suspiciously similar language, that Lucky Strike was their cigarette because it protected the throat from coughing and the waistline from an unhealthy appetite for fattening sweets.

But the decade's dominant and identifying trend in advertising was the increasing use of psychology, the deepening appeal to the secret emotions that motivated people to buy. If any single ad epitomized the trend and solemnized its acceptance, it was Ned Jordan's 173-word classic, "Somewhere West of Laramie" (opposite).

Jordan was a copywriter-turned-manufacturer: trained in the "nuts-and-bolts" school of auto advertising, he had given in to an urge to produce cars himself. One day he caught a glimpse of a custom-built roadster that showman Flo Ziegfeld had ordered for actress Billie Burke, and on the strength of rough sketches he raised $400,000, capital enough to buy parts and assemble some rakish, aluminum-bodied cars. Then Jordan launched his ad.

"Somewhere West of Laramie" broke all the rules. It offered no data on the Jordan's brakes or carburetor; it made no grandiose claims of power or elegance. But the ad firmly planted in the readers' minds a connection between the Jordan and a pleasant feeling of freedom, excitement, romantic adventure. That was enough. Jordan's cars were too costly to sell in volume, but, as Jordan later said, "We did make a lot of money awfully fast."

As the decade wore on, psychological insights—particularly the realization that fear was a wonderful persuader—were applied with increasing effectiveness, as shown by the ads on following pages. The practice was not, to be sure, admired by everyone. But even the malcontents agreed with a cheerful squib in the Kansas City Journal-Post: "Advertising and mass production are the twin cylinders that keep the motor of modern business in motion."

Somewhere West of Laramie

SOMEWHERE west of Laramie there's a broncho-busting, steer-roping girl who knows what I'm talking about.

She can tell what a sassy pony, that's a cross between greased lightning and the place where it hits, can do with eleven hundred pounds of steel and action when he's going high, wide and handsome.

The truth is—the Playboy was built for her.

Built for the lass whose face is brown with the sun when the day is done of revel and romp and race.

She loves the cross of the wild and the tame.

There's a savor of links about that car—of laughter and lilt and light—a hint of old loves—and saddle and quirt. It's a brawny thing—yet a graceful thing for the sweep o' the Avenue.

Step into the Playboy when the hour grows dull with things gone dead and stale.

Then start for the land of real living with the spirit of the lass who rides, lean and rangy, into the red horizon of a Wyoming twilight.

JORDAN

JORDAN MOTOR CAR COMPANY, Inc., Cleveland, Ohio

Jordan's famous ad used vague, poetic prose to glamorize its cars. Dubbed "word-magic," the new style became a standard tool for selling costly items.

The pause that refreshes

The Coca-Cola Company, Atlanta, Ga.

EACH busy day tends down hill from that top-of-the-morning feeling with which you begin. Don't whip yourself as the day begins to wear. Pause and refresh yourself with an ice-cold Coca-Cola, and be off to a fresh start. ▼ ▼ ▼ The wholesome refreshment of Coca-Cola has made it the one great drink of the millions. A perfect blend of many flavors, it has a flavor all its own—delicious to taste and, more than that, with a cool after-sense of refreshment. ▼ ▼ ▼ It is ready, cold and tingling, at fountains and refreshment stands around the corner from anywhere.

THE BEST SERVED DRINK IN THE WORLD
A pure drink of natural flavors served ice-cold in its own bottle—the distinctive Coca-Cola bottle. Every bottle is sterilized, filled and sealed air-tight by automatic machines, without the touch of human hands—insuring purity and wholesomeness.

IT HAD TO BE GOOD — OVER 8 MILLION A DAY — TO GET WHERE IT IS

I'll tell the world

They Satisfy

Chesterfield
CIGARETTES

Liggett & Myers Tobacco Co.

—and the blend can't be copied

"I'D WALK A MILE FOR A CAMEL"

—but a "MISS" is as Good as a MILE

SOLD ONLY IN SEALED TIN CANS—CONVENIENT TO OPEN AND USE

GOOD TO THE LAST DROP

ON THE GREAT WHITE FLEET

In the blue Caribbean

On the majestic ships of the United Fruit Company's Great White Fleet—famous for the excellence of their cuisine—with "Every Passenger a Guest"—Maxwell House Coffee is always served.

Sail on any of these super ships, and at your first meal, as you enjoy that delicious, fragrant coffee to the very last drop, call your waiter and ask: "What coffee is this?" He will tell you: "Maxwell House."

Go where you will—on fast, famous trains, to better hotels and restaurants, on great steamships, to the finest of private homes and to the humble cottage by the side of the road—and you will find within your cup of Maxwell House Coffee the fruit of a half century of search for flavor.

The finest coffees of the world are roasted, blended and packed in our six great plants, and sealed in the famous blue tin.

Also Maxwell House Tea.

CHEEK-NEAL COFFEE CO.,
Nashville,   Houston,   Jacksonville,   Richmond,   New York.

MAXWELL HOUSE COFFEE

Slogans old and new became familiar through repetition. Like others, "Good to the last drop" long outlived its creator: Theodore Roosevelt.

Defining the true meaning of the word "chic"

Coined in Paris to express originality plus taste, the word "chic" has come to mean many things to many people. In London, swagger; in America, pertness; in Japan, genuineness. The original and last meanings are the ones contained in the undoubted chic of Crane bathrooms. Always, originality and taste are found in Crane fixture designs and decorative suggestions; genuineness in the service given. At Crane Exhibit Rooms, you will find ideas for rooms as elaborate as the one above and others for the simplest cottage. Complete installation can be on monthly payments under the Crane Budget Plan. Let your architect help you plan. Buy from a Crane Qualified Contractor-Dealer, always a highly skilled registered or licensed master plumber or heating contractor.

Valves **CRANE** Fittings

FIXTURES, VALVES, FITTINGS, AND PIPING FOR DOMESTIC AND INDUSTRIAL USE

Crane Co., General Offices: 836 S. Michigan Ave., Chicago • 23 W. 44th St., New York • Branches and sales offices in one hundred and ninety-six cities

Snob Appeal

The consumer was often urged to buy a certain product because it was fashionable—i.e., preferred by people of wealth, position and savoir-faire. Many an ad depicted elegant folk in formal attire on some unlikely pilgrimage: down to the cellar to enjoy the clean heat provided by the American Radiator Company, into the kitchen to admire a General Electric refrigerator. In the case of bathrooms, the Crane Company suggested that its fixtures defined true "chic." Of course, bathrooms were only as fashionable as they were costly; the average wage earner might shell out three months' pay for the finest "shrine of cleanliness and health." In case he already had one such shrine, some ads strongly indicated that he needed another.

THE BEST SERVANT IN YOUR HOUSE

ABOVE is reproduced one of the modern efficiency kitchens shown in our book, "Your Kitchen as It Should Be." In this kitchen, designed by the well-known Chicago architects, Schmidt, Garden & Martin, space has been left for a Sellers Mastercraft Cabinet, and the additional storage cupboards built around it.

Among architects of standing it is increasingly the practice to make a Sellers Cabinet a basic part of the kitchen plan. They recognize, as do well-informed builders and housewives, that a built-in cabinet costs practically twice as much as a Sellers, and lacks all those exclusive features that make the Sellers a marvel of convenience—the Automatic Lowering Flour Bin, Porceliron Table Top, Automatic Base Shelf Extender, Extending Table Drawer Section, Dust-Proof Base Top, Plush-Lined Silverware Drawer and other features.

Any dealer will show you the Sellers and its "Fifteen Famous Features." Most of them will gladly arrange terms to suit your income. Write for nearest dealer's name and our new book of efficiency kitchen plans.

G. I. SELLERS & SONS COMPANY, Elwood, Indiana
Canadian Branch: Sellers Kitchen Cabinets, Brantford, Canada

SELLERS
KITCHEN CABINETS

From a painting by WALTER BIGGS

© ARCO, 1925

What! Company in the cellar!

YES, INDEED. Invite them down. No reason why they shouldn't see the cellar if you have an IDEAL TYPE A HEAT MACHINE.

The IDEAL TYPE A, being itself so clean and handsome, has caused hundreds of cellars to be cleaned up and dressed up; it has turned the wasted part of the home into a usable and useful part.

"It is the most efficient heating plant on the market, and is very easily kept clean," writes Leland H. Lyon, New York architect, whose home is in New Rochelle, New York.

"Many men, when visiting me, are amazed that the room in which the IDEAL TYPE A stands should be so entirely free from gas or dust. I have several electrical devices in the same room and there is, at no time, any appreciable amount of dust on the motors."

Why not, like Mr. Lyon, add another floor—the cellar—to the serviceable part of your home? The IDEAL TYPE A will do it, *and will pay back the cost of the improvement in the fuel it saves.*

Send to either address below for an illustrated booklet which tells the whole story.

AMERICAN RADIATOR COMPANY
IDEAL Boilers and AMERICAN Radiators for every heating need

It hasn't a single belt, fan or drain pipe....

It always works perfectly and never needs oiling . . . .

ONE of the first things that made me favor this General Electric Refrigerator was the fact that it was so unusually quiet. And I liked the idea of never having to oil it. All you have to do is plug it into an electric outlet . . . and then you can forget it. It hasn't any belts, drains, fans, or stuffing boxes.

But, of course, the thing that appeals to me most is the way it has cut my housekeeping job. I only market twice a week now, because I have plenty of space and just the right temperature to keep all sorts of foods in perfect condition.

We go away for week-ends without having to worry about ice. Everything is ready for use when we get back.

Cooking has become easier, too. Desserts, which used to be the most difficult part of the dinner to prepare, now are beautifully simple —and ever so much more attractive.

Expensive to run? Not a bit. It uses very little current to make all the ice we need and give us perfect refrigeration. And, do you know, it's quite remarkable the way the top of this box never gets dusty. The circulation of air through those coils seems to drive the dust away.

′ ′ ′ ′

For fifteen years the vast laboratories of General Electric have been busy developing a simplified refrigerator that would be about as easy to operate as an electric fan . . . and almost as portable. Four thousand models of nineteen different types were built, field-tested and improved before this new-day refrigerator was brought to its present simplicity and efficiency.

You will want to see the models. Let us send you the address of the dealer who has them on display and booklet 11-J, which is interesting and completely descriptive.

Electric Refrigeration Department
of General Electric Company

Hanna Building   Cleveland, Ohio

Refrigerator

GENERAL ELECTRIC

Cheesecake in the Ads

*As changing fashions exposed more and more of
the female form, the trend was recorded—
and accelerated—by daring advertisers. Among the
leaders was the Holeproof Hosiery Company,
whose ads helped transform silk stockings from a
sheer luxury to an impractical necessity.
The display of silk-clad limbs proved to be such an
eye-catcher that it was used to advertise many
other products. This practice called forth
a facetious protest from a female wit, who said of
mail-order ads, "If you accept the invitation to
'Sign Here Today,' under a pair of silk stockings,
what a miscellany of articles will come
parcel-posting unexpectedly into your front hall.
Beaver board for walls and ceilings! Electric
washing machines! A new kind of raisin pie!"*

Holeproof Hosiery

COLES PHILLIPS

HOLEPROOF is the hosiery of lustrous beauty and fine texture that wears so well. It is not surprising, therefore, that it is selected by many people who can afford to pay far more for their hose, but who prefer the Holeproof combination of style and serviceability at such reasonable prices.

Obtainable in Pure Silk, Silk Faced, and Lusterized Lisle styles for men, women and children in the season's popular colors. If your dealer cannot supply you, write for price list and illustrated booklet.

HOLEPROOF HOSIERY COMPANY, Milwaukee, Wisconsin

Holeproof Hosiery Company of Canada, Limited, London, Ontario   © H. H. Co.

Collapse and Confusion on the Market

In November 1929, soon after the stock market crash, a New York policeman found a bedraggled parrot. In a fitting epitaph to the disaster, the bird kept squawking, "More margin! More margin!"

The lack of more margin was the straw that broke the back of the Big Bull Market and signaled the end of the Coolidge-Hoover prosperity. Before the market cracked, stocks were not only priced far above their real value; they were being bought for a marginal down payment of as little as 10 per cent, with the bulk of the purchase price financed by brokers' loans. As stock prices slumped, overextended investors were required to put up additional margin, and many could produce the capital only by selling off shares at distress prices. This drove the market into a steeper, broader descent—and redoubled the brokers' demands for margin. Between late October and mid-November, stocks lost more than 40 per cent of their total valuation—a drop of $30 billion in paper values.

Those few weeks were a nightmare. Market-wise reporters struggled in vain to describe adequately the pandemonium on the stock exchange floor. Broker Fred Schwed later wrote ironically: "Like all life's rich emotional experiences, the full flavor of losing important money cannot be conveyed by literature." Only slowly, as personal anecdotes fleshed out the appalling statistics, did the scope of the Crash become amply evident.

One woman, presented by her broker with an enormous bill for more margin, cried out in bewilderment, "How could I lose $100,000? I never *had* $100,000." Facing the mad scramble to obtain margin money, pawnbrokers had to turn away hundreds seeking loans on jewelry.

October 29, when stocks suffered their worst losses *(opposite)*, was catastrophic for almost everyone but a shrewd (and possibly apocryphal) messenger boy. Noting that a big block of White Sewing Machine stock was being offered at any price with no takers, he allegedly snapped it up at a dollar a share.

In an effort to bolster confidence, John D. Rockefeller announced, "My son and I have for some days been purchasing sound common stocks." A spirited rejoinder came from one of many hard-hit celebrities, comedian Eddie Cantor: "Sure, who else had any money left?"

The president of Union Cigar, stunned when his company's stock plummeted from $113.50 to four dollars in a day, fell or jumped to his death from the ledge of a New York hotel. Tales of suicide became standard fare in the mythology of the Crash. Actually, the suicide rate was higher in the few months before the Crash than in those just after it. Still, thousands of people had lost everything but their lives, and there was much truth to one man's remark that, while Jerusalem had only one Wailing Wall, "in Wall Street every wall is wet with tears."

In the aftermath, the country seemed to pause with bated breath while its leaders formed opinions. Their confident verdicts were not long in coming. Said President Hoover: "The fundamental business of the country, that is, production and distribution of commodities, is on a sound and prosperous basis." Statements by economists and businessmen pronounced stock prices "stabilized," the Crash "wholesome," the outlook "favorable."

But certain conditions, visible for months to anyone who put aside his rose-colored glasses, told quite another story: the economy was basically unsound. Banks and corporations were structurally weak and in many cases undermined by skullduggery and fraud. America's trade policies were self-defeating. The market for consumer goods was both glutted and untapped: 90 per cent of the nation's wealth was concentrated in the hands of only 13 per cent of the people; meanwhile, large depressed segments of society—among them farmers, textile workers and coal miners—lacked sufficient income to buy much more than their minimal needs. In its relation to these and other unhealthy symptoms, the stock market crash was far more than a private retribution for greedy speculators. It was a clear warning for all.

Yet most of the pundits held that prospects were bright, and everyone wanted to believe the good word. Tentatively reassured, people resumed their business pursuits, tried to recapture their boom-time zest for getting and spending. But somehow things were not quite the same.

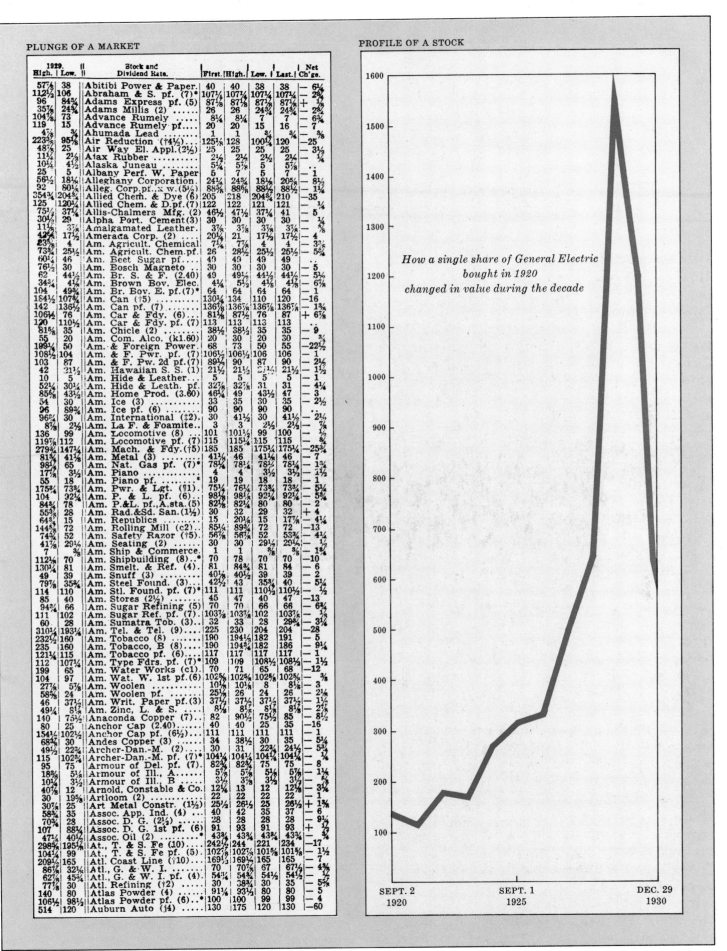

1929. High.	Low.	Stock and Dividend Rate.	First.	High.	Low.	Last.	Net Ch'ge.
57⅞	38	Abitibi Power & Paper.	40	40	38	38	— 6⅞
112½	106	Abraham & S. pf. (7)*	107¼	107¼	107¼	107¼	— 2⅞
96	84¾	Adams Express pf. (5)	87⅛	87⅞	87⅞	87⅞	+ ½
35⅝	24¾	Adams Millis (2)	26	26	24¾	24¾	— 2⅞
104⅞	73	Advance Rumely	8¼	8¼	7	7	— 6¾
119	15	Advance Rumely pf....	20	20	15	16	— 7
4⅞	¾	Ahumada Lead	1	1	¾	¾	— ⅜
223⅜	95⅝	Air Reduction (†4½)...	125⅛	128	100¼	120	—25
48⅞	25	Air Way El. Appl.(2½)	25	25	25	25	— 3¼
11¼	2½	Ajax Rubber	2½	2½	2½	2¼	— ¼
10¼	4½	Alaska Juneau	5¼	5⅞	5	5⅞	..
25	5	Albany Perf. W. Paper	5	7	5	7	— 1
56½	18¼	Alleghany Corporation.	24¼	24¾	18¼	20⅝	— 8½
92	80¼	Alleg. Corp.pf.,x w.(5½)	88⅝	88⅝	88½	88½	— 1¾
354¾	204¾	Allied Chem. & Dye (6)	205	218	204¾	210	—35
125	120¼	Allied Chem. & D.pf.(7)	122	122	121	121	— ¼
75¼	37¾	Allis-Chalmers Mfg. (2)	46½	47½	37¼	41	— 5
30½	29	Alpha Port. Cement(3)	30	30	30	30	— ¼
11½	3⅞	Amalgamated Leather.	3⅞	3⅞	3⅞	3⅞	..
42⅝	17½	Amerada Corp. (2)	20¼	21	17½	17½	— 4
23⅝	4	Am. Agricult. Chemical	7¼	7⅞	4	4	— 3⅜
73⅝	25½	Am. Agricult. Chem.pf.	26	28½	25½	25½	— 5¾
60¼	46	Am. Beet Sugar pf....	49	49	49	49	..
76½	30	Am. Bosch Magneto ..	30	30	30	30	— 5
62	44½	Am. Br. S. & F. (2.40)	49	49½	44½	44½	— 5½
34¾	4¾	Am. Brown Bov. Elec.	4¾	5½	4⅞	4⅞	— 6⅞
104	49⅜	Am. Br. Bov. E. pf.(7)*	64	64	64	64	— 1
184½	107⅞	Am. Can (†5)	130¼	134	110	120	—16
142	136½	Am. Can pf. (7)	136⅞	136¼	136⅞	136¼	— 1¾
106½	76	Am. Car & Fdy. (6)...	81⅛	87½	76	87	+ 6⅞
120	110½	Am. Car & Fdy. pf. (7)	113	113	113	113	..
81⅝	35	Am. Chicle (2)	38½	38½	35	35	— 9
55	20	Am. Com. Alco. (k1.60)	20	30	20	30	— ¾
199¼	50	Am. & Foreign Power.	68	73	50	55	—22½
108½	104	Am. & F. Pwr. pf. (7)	106½	106½	106	106	— 1
103	87	Am. & F. Pw. 2d pf.(7)	89½	90	87	90	— 2½
42	21½	Am. Hawaiian S. S. (1)	21½	21½	21¼	21½	— 1½
10	5	Am. Hide & Leather..	5	5	5	5	— 1
52¼	30¼	Am. Hide & Leath. pf.	32⅞	32⅞	31	31	— 4¼
85⅝	43½	Am. Home Prod. (3.60)	46¼	49	43½	47	— 3
54	30	Am. Ice (3)	33	35	30	35	— 2½
96	89¾	Am. Ice pf. (6)	90	90	90	90	..
96¾	30	Am. International (†2).	30	41½	30	41½	— 2½
8⅞	2½	Am. La F. & Foamite..	3	3	2½	2½	— ⅞
136	99	Am. Locomotive (8) ..	101	101½	99	100	— ½
119⅞	112	Am. Locomotive pf. (7)	115	115¼	115	115	— ¾
279¾	147¼	Am. Mach. & Fdy.(†5)	185	185	175¼	175¼	—25¾
81½	41⅛	Am. Metal (3)	41½	46	41½	46	— 7
98¼	65	Am. Nat. Gas pf. (7)*	78¼	78¼	78¼	78¼	— 1¾
17⅞	3½	Am. Piano	4	4	3½	3½	— 1½
55	18	Am. Piano pf. ......*	19	19	18	18	— 1
175¾	73¾	Am. Pwr. & Lgt. (†1).	75¼	76¼	73¾	73¾	— 5¼
104	92¼	Am. P. & L. pf. (6) ..	98⅞	98⅛	92¼	92¼	— 5¾
84½	78	Am. P.&L. pf.,A,sta.(5)	82⅞	82¼	80	80	— 2
55⅜	28	Am. Rad.&Sd. San.(1½)	30	32	29	32	+ 4
64⅜	15	Am. Republics	15	20¼	15	17⅞	— 4¼
144⅝	72	Am. Rolling Mill (c2).	85¼	89¾	72	72	—13
74½	52	Am. Safety Razor (†5)	56⅞	56⅞	52	53¾	— 4¼
41⅞	29¼	Am. Seating (2)	30	30	29½	29¼	— ½
7	⅜	Am. Ship & Commerce.	1	1	⅞	⅞	— 1⅛
112⅛	70	Am. Shipbuilding (8)..*	70	78	70	70	—10
130¼	81	Am. Smelt. & Ref. (4).	81	84½	81	84	— 6
49	39	Am. Snuff (3)	40½	40½	39	39	— 2
79¾	35⅝	Am. Steel Found. (3)...	42½	43	35¾	40	— 5¼
114	110	Am. Stl. Found. (7)*	111	111	110½	110½	— ½
85	40	Am. Stores (2½)	45	47	40	47	—13
94¾	66	Am. Sugar Refining (5)	70	70	66	66	— 6¾
111	102	Am. Sugar Ref. pf. (7)	103⅞	103⅞	102	103⅞	— ¾
60	28	Am. Sumatra Tob. (3).	32	33	28	29¾	— 3¼
310¼	193¼	Am. Tel. & Tel. (9)....	225	230	204	204	—28
232½	160	Am. Tobacco (8)	190	194½	182	191	— 5
235	160	Am. Tobacco, B (8)....	190	194¾	182	186	— 9¼
121¼	115	Am. Tobacco pf. (6)...	117	117	117	117	— 1
112	107¼	Am. Type Fdrs. pf. (7)*	109	109	108½	108½	— 1½
199	65	Am. Water Works (c1).	70	71	65	68	—12
104	97	Am. Wat. W. 1st pf.(6)	102⅝	102⅝	102⅝	102⅝	— ⅜
27⅞	5⅞	Am. Woolen	10⅛	10⅛	8	8⅛	— 3
58⅝	24	Am. Woolen pf.	25½	26	24	26	— 2¼
46	37½	Am. Writ. Paper pf.(3)	37½	37½	37½	37½	— 1½
49¼	8¼	Am. Zinc, L. & S. ...	8⅞	8⅞	8⅛	8⅛	— 2⅞
140	75½	Anaconda Copper (7)..	82	90½	75½	85	— 8½
80	25	Anchor Cap (2.40).....	40	40	25	35	—16
154¼	102½	Anchor Cap pf. (6½)...	111	111	111	111	— 1
68¾	30	Andes Copper (3)	34	38½	30	35	— 5¼
49½	22¾	Archer-Dan.-M. (2)...	30	31	22¾	24½	— 5¾
115	102¾	Archer-Dan.-M. pf. (7)*	104¼	104¼	104¼	104¼	— ¼
95	75	Armour of Del. pf. (7).	82½	82½	75	75	— 8
18⅜	5⅛	Armour of Ill., A	5⅞	5⅞	5⅛	5⅞	— 1¼
10¼	3½	Armour of Ill., B	3½	3⅞	3½	3⅞	— ⅝
40⅞	12	Arnold, Constable & Co.	12¼	13	12	12⅞	— 3¼
30	19⅝	Artloom (2)	22	22	22	22	— 1
30⅞	25	Art Metal Constr. (1½)	25½	26½	25	26½	+ 1⅜
58⅝	35	Assoc. App. Ind. (4) ..	40	42	35	37	— 6
70⅜	28	Assoc. D. G. (2½)	28	28	28	28	— 9½
107	88¼	Assoc. D. G. 1st pf. (6)	91	93	91	93	+ ½
47¼	40½	Assoc. Oil (2) ....*	43¾	43¾	43¾	43¾	— ¾
298⅝	195⅝	At., T. & S. Fe (10)..	242½	244	221	234	—17
104¼	99	At., T. & S. Fe pf. (5).	102⅝	102⅞	101⅝	101⅝	— 1½
209½	165	Atl. Coast Line (†10)..	169¼	169½	165	165	— 7
86¾	32¼	Atl., G. & W. I.	70	70½	67	67½	— 4⅞
62⅞	45¾	Atl., G. & W. I. pf. (4).	54¾	54½	54½	54½	— ⅜
77⅝	30	Atl. Refining (†2)	30	38¾	30	35	— 5⅞
140	80	Atlas Powder (4)	91¼	93½	80	80	— 5
106½	98½	Atlas Powder pf. (6).. *	100	100	99	99	— 4
514	120	Auburn Auto (j4)	130	175	120	130	—60

How a single share of General Electric bought in 1920 changed in value during the decade

SEPT. 2 1920	SEPT. 1 1925	DEC. 29 1930

Black Tuesday, October 29, 1929, cost the stock list (left) $14 billion; the crash sent General Electric, a typical loser, plummeting (chart).

WORST STOCK CRASH STEMMED BY BANKS; 12,894,650-SHARE DAY SWAMPS MARKET; LEADERS CONFER, FIND CONDITIONS SOUND

FINANCIERS EASE TENSION

Five Wall Street Bankers Hold Two Meetings at Morgan Office.

Wall Street Optimistic After Stormy Day; Clerical Work May Force Holiday Tomorrow

Confidence in the soundness of the stock market structure, notwithstanding the upheaval of the last few days, was voiced last night by bankers and other financial leaders. Sentiment as expressed by the heads of some of the largest banking institutions and by industrial executives as well was distinctly cheerful and the feeling was general that the worst had been seen. Wall Street ended the day in an optimistic frame of mind.

The opinion of brokers was unanimous that the selling had got ... inherent weakness in the market

LOSSES RECOVERED IN PART

Upward Trend Start With 200,000-Share Order for Steel.

TICKERS LAG FOUR HOU

STOCKS GAIN AS MARKET IS BANKERS PLEDGE CONTINU HOOVER SAYS BUSINESS B

President Hoover Issues a Statement of Reassurance On Continued Prosperity of Fundamental Business

Special to The New York Times.

WASHINGTON, Oct. 25.—A reassuring statement that the fundamental business of the country was on a sound and prosperous basis was made by President Hoover at the White House this afternoon. It was made in reply to questions by newspaper men asking his opinion on the possible effect on the nation's prosperity of yesterday's collapse in the stock market.

Prior to his announcement, the President is ... received detailed reports of th... the current ...

Weird Roar Surges From Exchange Floor During Trading in a Reco

BROKERS IN UPROAR AS MARKET BOILS

1,000 Mill Madly on Floor of Exchange and Thunder of Voices Is Heard Outside.

FURIOUS PACE BEFORE GONG

Then Perspiring Traders With Torn Collars Stand Limply or Jump and Laugh.

CROWDS SURGE IN ...

Time to Buy Stocks, Says Raskob; Sees Only Temporary Effect on Business

John J. Raskob, one of the country's leading industrial and political leaders, declared last night in a statement to THE NEW YORK TIMES that many stocks are selling at bargain prices and that he and his friends are buyers of stocks. It may be stated in this connection that Mr.

"In a panic, whether in a theatre fire or the stock market, people lose their heads and go too far, which always results in needless and unnecessary suffering.

"Prudent investors are now buying stocks in huge quantities and will profit handsomely when this hysteria is over and our people have opportunity in the calmer moments to appreciate the great stability of business by reason of the sound fundamental economic conditions existing in this great country.

"The pendulum has swung too far. The list is filled with bargains and I are all buying

... list is filled with stocks selling at real bargain prices.

SENATORS STIRRED BY MARKET BREAK

King Presses His Proposal for Investigation of Federal Reserve System.

GLASS SEES VIEWS BACKED

...lans to Offer Measure for Tax on Sales as Tariff Bill Rider— Action Unlikely Till Decem

in stirring up interest in his pending resolution offered last May for an investigation of the Federal Reserve System. He said he would insist upon action by the Senate Banking and Currency Committee in the December session.

Immediate Inquiry Unlikely.

Senator Norbeck of South Dakota, chairman of that committee, declared that the committee apparently would favor an inquiry in the regular session, but there was little probability that it would be recommended in the present session. At this time the Senate is absorbed in the tariff bill.

Senator King said:

"Gambling in stock has become a national disease. This malady reaches all classes of people, from preachers to stable boys. Only a short time ago in all circles every one was talk-

Special to The New York Ti...

...ASHINGTON, Oct. 24.—T r collapse of the stock ...ay caused a revival in the ...suggestions for legislative ...rdment of the National ...lits used in the stock ...ong with such proposals ...Senators advocated an ...stigation of the Federal ...ystem, as proposed

Crowds See M

CROWDS AT TICKERS SEE FORTUNES WANE

Other Investors Sit Silently in

STOCK PRICES SLUMP $14,000,000,000 IN NATION-WIDE STAMPEDE TO UNLOAD; BANKERS TO SUPPORT MARKET TOD

Sixteen Leading Issues Down $2,893,520,108; Tel. & Tel. and Steel Among Heaviest Losers

A shrinkage of $2,893,520,108 in the open market value of the shares of sixteen representative companies resulted from yesterday's sweeping decline on the New York Stock Exchange.

American Telephone and Telegraph was the heaviest loser, $448,905,162 having been lopped off of its total value. United States Steel common, traditional bellwether of the stock market, made its greatest nose-dive in recent years by falling from a high of 202½ to a low of 185. In a feeble last-minute rally it snapped back to 186, at which it closed, showing a net loss of 17½ points. This represented for the 8,131,055 shares of common stock outstanding a total loss in value of $142,293,446.

In the following table are shown the day's net depreciation in the outstanding shares of the sixteen companies referred to:

Issues.	Shares Listed.	Losses in Points. 10%	Depreciation
American Radiator	10,096,289	10½	$104,748,997
American Tel. & Tel.	13,203,093	34	448,905,162
Commonwealth & Southern	30,764,468	3½	96,138,962
Columbia Gas & Electric.	8,477,307	22	186,500,754
Consolidated Gas	11,451,188	20	229,023,760
DuPont E. I.	10,322,481	16½	160,030,625
Eastman Kodak	2,229,703	41¾	342,545,490
General Electric	7,211,484	47½	293,625,000
General Motors	43,500,000	6¾	108,497.0
International Nickel	13,777,408	7½	104,914,0
New York Central	4,637,086	22⅝	198,749,1
Standard Oil of New Jersey	24,843,643	8	174,615,4
Union Carbide & Carbon.	8,730,173	20	142,293,
United States Steel	8,131,055	17½	111,881,
United Gas Improvement	18,646,835	6	88,682,
...inghouse Elec. & Mfg.	2,589,265	34½	$2,893,520

... table are typical, but

PREMIER ISSUES HA

Unexpected Tor Liquidation Rocks Marl

DAY'S SALES

STOCKS MOUNT IN STRONG ALL-DAY RALLY; ROCKEFELLER BUYING HEARTENS MARKET; 2-DAY CLOSING ORDERED TO EASE STRAIN

Stocks Recover Nearly Half of Two Days' Losses; Total Gain in 16 Leading Issues Is $2,367,986,611

A group of sixteen representative stocks, which lost $2,893,520,108 in open market value in Monday's slump on the New York Stock Exchange and which showed almost as great a depreciation in Tuesday's break, recovered $2,367,986,611 in value yesterday, or nearly half of the aggregate loss of the group for the two-day break.

GAINS UP TO 36 POINTS

Prices Climb Steadily as 10,727,320 Shares Are Traded in Da...

Weary Throngs in Brokers' Offices Ch

EXHAUSTED CROWDS CHEER STOCK RISE

Joy Supplants Fear in 1,000 Brokers' Rooms as Tickers Record Turning of Tide.

EXCHANGE HOLIDAY HAILED

Tired Customers Look Forward to Sleep Long Deferred. Clerks to

Weary Runners Nap on Bank's Marble Floor; Mitchell Orders Chairs Brought for Them

The results of the terrific strain of a succession of record-breaking days culminating in Tuesday's enormous turnover of 16,410,030 shares have extended to all sections of Wall Street's personnel. Nowhere was this more strikingly illustrated than in the scenes which took place on the main banking floor of the National City Bank at 55 Wall Street.

Hundreds of weary messengers, their hands and pockets crammed with bundles of securities worth hun-dreds of thousands of dollars crowd-

the bank, it would have been comparatively simple for some one to steal a wallet full of negotiable stocks from some sleeping messenger.

Mr. Mitchell quickly ordered the guards to rouse the messengers and had camp chairs brought in for them to sit upon. For the rest of the afternoon the main floor of the bank resembled a drowsy prayer meeting with the runners playing a species of "marching to Jerusalem" as they gradually edged closer and closer to the loan windows.

In other banks similar scenes were enacted on a somewhat smaller scale. The unprecedented volume of trading

ROBINSON BLAMES THE REPUBLICANS

Charges Hoover, Mellon and Coolidge Fostered Era of Disastrous Speculation.

SAYS NONE ACTED ON BREAK

"High Priests of Prosperity" at Fault in Their Optimistic State-

Women T Say Th

The women took up the pa... seemed yester... returning to b... uptown office... firms, irritable... 3 o'clock the... remarks was...forever.

Stock broke... women specu... losers. Many... most worried... They pushed... crowded room... quotations a... brokers for... In one office... chins asked a... a quotation,... marked: "Y... gentleman,?...

Another wo... into the sam... loudly that s... seemed prou... and went off.

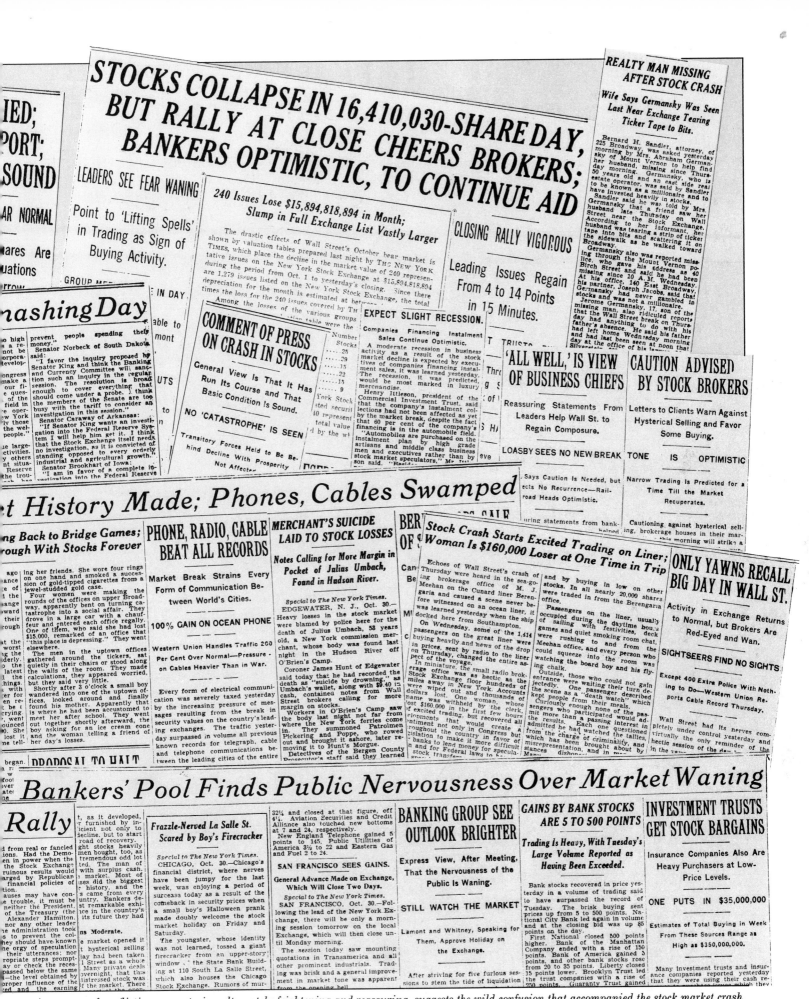

A montage of conflicting news stories, alternately frightening and reassuring, suggests the wild confusion that accompanied the stock market crash.

The Sports Stars

All cameras are focused on Babe Ruth at the 1921 World Series.

An Era of Giants

I see them walk by in a dream—Dempsey and Cobb and Ruth,

Tunney and Sande and Jones—Johnson and Matty and Young—

Alex and Tilden and Thorpe—was there a flash of youth

That gave us a list like this, when our first tributes were sung?

GRANTLAND RICE

This was the heroic era of American sports. Attendance at athletic events broke all records, and the champions of sport were known and loved throughout the land. "If St. Paul were living today," a prominent Methodist minister declared, "he would know Babe Ruth's batting average and what yardage Red Grange made."

And that applied to many others besides Ruth and Grange. Jack Dempsey, the grim Manassa Mauler, came out of the West to give boxing its first million-dollar gates. Bobby Jones and Bill Tilden took golf and tennis away from the country-club crowd and made them "important" sports. Swimmer Gertrude Ederle, Helen Wills, a tennis player, and golfer Glenna Collett showed that a woman's place was also in the sports pages.

One reason for the heightened interest in sport was the sudden emergence of the sports writer as a major figure on the literary scene—men such as Grantland Rice, Damon Runyon, Ring Lardner, Paul Gallico, John Kieran and Westbrook Pegler. These experts were occasionally assisted by outsiders like H. L. Mencken and even George Bernard Shaw. (Shaw described the game of baseball as a combination of the "best features of that primitive form of cricket known as Tip and Run with those of lawn tennis, Puss-in-the-Corner, and Handel's *Messiah*.")

The great writers recorded the deeds of the great athletes. One early beneficiary was that giant of giants, Babe Ruth. "After the Black Sox scandal," wrote W. O. McGeehan, "Babe Ruth with his bat pounded baseball back into popularity. He swings with the utmost sincerity. When he hits the ball it goes into wide-open spaces. When he misses, he misses with vehement sincerity."

By 1927, when he hit his high-water mark of 60 home runs, Babe Ruth was a better-known American to most foreigners than Calvin Coolidge, and he rivaled the dashing Prince of Wales as the most photographed man in the world. Kieran was moved to this bit of hero-worshipping doggerel, typical of the sports-page exaggeration of the era: "My voice may be loud above the crowd / And my words just a bit uncouth, / But I'll stand and shout till the last man's out: / 'There never was a guy like Ruth!' "

The fact that the Babe was himself a bit uncouth—a wencher, imbiber, and notorious violator of training rules—bothered neither the writers nor the fans. He was simply the greatest ballplayer who ever lived, and he symbolized as no other man ever did the love affair that existed between the American public and the athletes of the 1920s.

Paul Gallico wrote of Ruth: "There has always been a magic about that gross, ugly, coarse, Gargantuan figure of a man and everything he did."

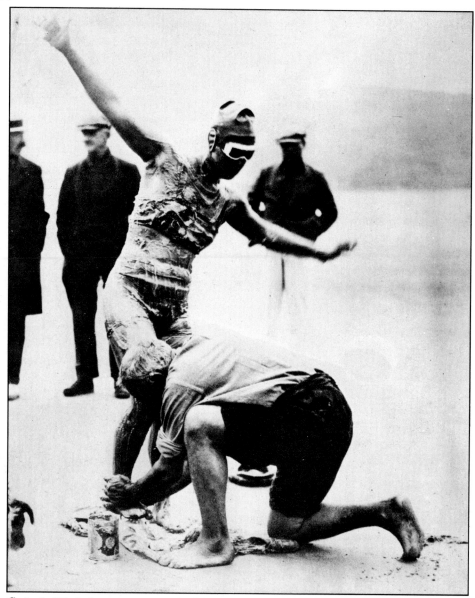

Gertrude Ederle dons grease to ward off the cold before swimming the English Channel in 1926.

The Supreme Swimmers

In 1926, when 19-year-old Gertrude Ederle swam the English Channel, it was front-page news across the nation. Not only was "Our Trudy" the first woman to conquer the Channel, but her time—14 hours and 31 minutes—was almost two hours faster than the men's record. She was lionized with a huge ticker-tape parade when she returned to New York. The excerpt at right, from the *New York Herald Tribune,* shows the esteem in which Trudy was held at her peak. But by the following year she was slipping into obscurity and the headlines once more belonged to handsome swimming idol Johnny Weissmuller *(opposite).* Between 1921 and 1929—when he "retired" from competition at the age of 24—Weissmuller set some 67 records.

If there is one woman who can make the swim, it is this girl, with the shoulders and back of Jack Dempsey and the frankest and bravest pair of eyes that ever looked into a face. She told me of her last attempt, when she swam for an hour on instinct alone, blinded, deaf and only half conscious. She remembered only the humor of the trip. This girl keeps her even temper. I felt that I would sooner be in that tug the day she starts than at the ringside of the greatest fight or at the arena of the greatest game in the world, for this, in my opinion, is to be the greatest sports story in the world.

W. O. McGEEHAN

Johnny Weissmuller, never beaten in any free-style race from 100 yards to a half mile, set a world record for 100 meters at the 1924 Olympic Games.

Red Grange, shown as a pro player, said, "The same fellows who advised me not to play professional wouldn't lend me a dollar if I were broke."

The Rock and the Redhead

Until the '20s, a fair number of Eastern sports writers believed that the only brand of college football worth writing about was played on the gridirons of Harvard, Yale and Princeton. And then along came Knute Rockne and Red Grange out of the Midwest to change their minds.

Rockne's superbly coached Notre Dame teams won 105 games and lost only 12 between 1919 and 1931. His locker-room exhortations became football lore; but his real renown rested on his ability to find—and make—fine football players. Four of the best were on his 1924 team; after that year's victory over Army, while groping for words to describe the small, swift Notre Dame backfield, Grantland Rice typed: "Outlined against a blue-gray October sky, the Four Horsemen rode again. In dramatic lore they are known as Famine, Pestilence, Destruction and Death. These are only aliases. Their real names are Stuhldreher, Miller, Crowley and Layden."

But even the best players Rockne could produce were overshadowed by Red Grange, the "Galloping Ghost" of Illinois. A three-time All-American, Grange helped dedicate Illinois' new stadium in 1924 by personally demolishing a fine Michigan team with touchdown runs of 95, 67, 55 and 45 yards the first four times he carried the ball. Within hours after he stripped off his famous No. 77 jersey for the last time in 1925, Grange signed a contract to play professionally. "I do not like football well enough to play it for nothing," he explained. Playing it for about $1,000 a minute, Grange was a millionaire in just three years.

A fter his team had taken a first-half shellacking and sat waiting for the blast, Rockne merely poked his head in the door of the dressing room and remarked quietly, "Oh, excuse me, ladies! I thought this was the Notre Dame team."   PAUL GALLICO

What a football player—this man Red Grange. He is melody and symphony. He is crashing sound. He is brute force.

DAMON RUNYON

KNUTE ROCKNE

139

At 32, Dempsey still packed a wallop in his right, called "Iron Mike."

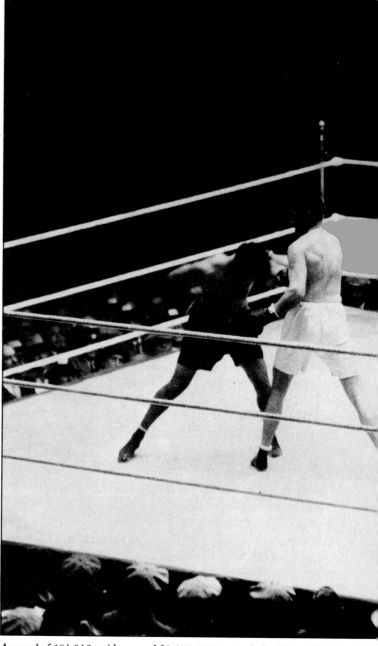

A crowd of 104,942 paid a record $2,658,600 to watch the fight, while about 50

Dempsey's Last Shot

The greatest prize fight of the decade occurred at Chicago's Soldiers' Field on September 22, 1927. The principals were the aging challenger, Jack Dempsey, and heavyweight champion Gene Tunney, a methodical boxer four years younger who liked to quote Shakespeare.

Dempsey and Tunney had met once before, a year earlier, when Dempsey had been the cocky champion, Tunney the challenger. But when that fight was over, Dempsey was a battered loser. His refusal to alibi his defeat

was cherished by ring fans. ("What happened?" asked his dismayed wife, actress Estelle Taylor. "Honey," said Dempsey, "I forgot to duck.")

The 1927 rematch, billed as "The Battle of the Ages," actually was a dull fight until the seventh round. Then Dempsey, with his old vigor, made a bid for victory—described at right in a *New York Times* story—only to commit a blunder that resulted in a controversy: did Tunney get the benefit of a "long count" or did he win fair and square?

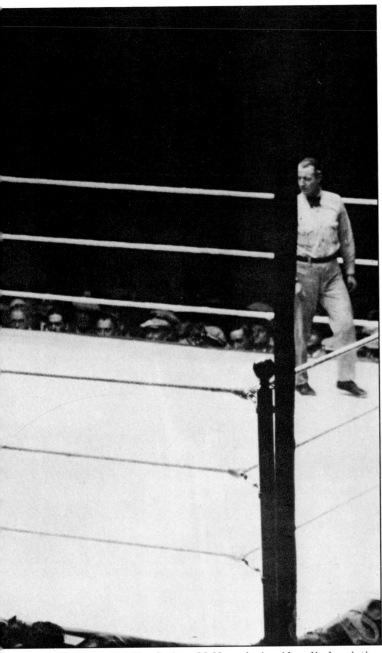

million Americans listened to Graham McNamee's ringside radio description.

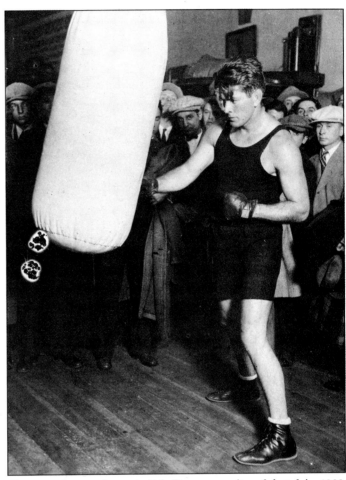

Tunney, whose goal was to lick Dempsey, quit undefeated in 1928.

Dempsey, plunging in recklessly, suddenly lashed a long, wicked left to the jaw. This he followed with a right to the jaw, the old "Iron Mike" as deadly as ever, and quickly drove another left hook to the jaw, under which Tunney toppled like a falling tree. The challenging ex-champion stood there in his own corner, the characteristic Dempsey snarl o'erspreading his countenance, his expression saying more plainly than words: "Get up and I'll knock you down again." Finally Dempsey took cognizance of the referee's frantic motions and sped across the ring to a neutral corner. But three or four, or possibly five precious seconds elapsed. Tunney got to his feet with the assistance of ring ropes and with visible effort at the count of "nine." He was groggy. But Dempsey was wild, a floundering plodding mankiller as Tunney, backpedaling for dear life, took to full flight. The former champion stopped dead in his tracks in mid-ring and with a smile spreading over his scowling face, motioned disgustedly for Tunney to come on and fight. But Tunney was playing his own game and it was a winning game.

JAMES P. DAWSON

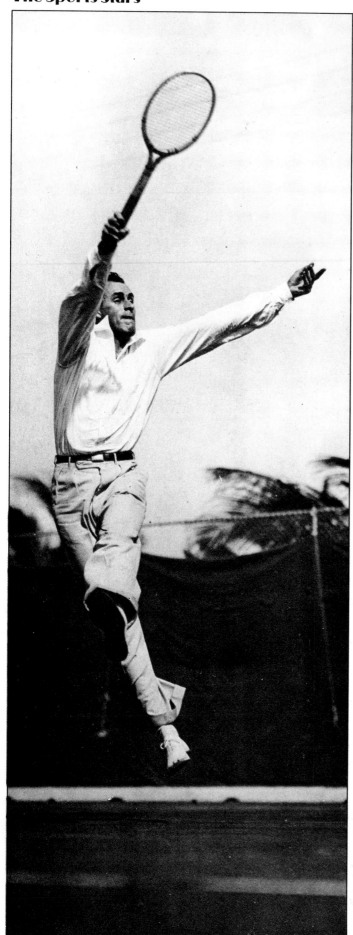

A slim six-footer, Bill Tilden never weighed more than 165 pounds.

The Reign of Big Bill

William Tatem Tilden II, the greatest tennis player of the decade, once wrote: "The player owes the gallery as much as an actor owes an audience." It was typical of Big Bill to link tennis and the theater, the two worlds he loved most. Purists might complain that he did too much acting on the court—holding aloft an injured finger or playing with his sweater on for a set or two before peeling it off for the inevitable blazing finish—but the new generation of tennis fans that Tilden created loved every scene. Ironically, Big Bill was probably a better actor on the tennis court than he was on the stage. He spent a small fortune bankrolling plays in which he was the star. But none of them had tennis scenes, which may explain why all of them were flops.

Big Bill was all of 27 years old, a ripe old age in competitive tennis, when he won his first national singles championship in 1920 and he was still going strong when he added championship No. 7 at the age of 36. A famous columnist, writing in *Collier's* in 1922 after watching Tilden come from two sets down to defeat "Little Bill" Johnston, his most persistent rival, caught the full flavor of Tilden's artistic temperament in the following excerpt.

It seems as though Tilden often says to himself: "This is going to be a hard match." Coming to play, he finds it easy. So he makes it hard. He loses a set or two, usually electrifying the gallery in the winning of the match. "Playing to the stands," say his legion of sneering commentators. I am certain that he would play exactly the same game, saying the same "Oh, rotten" when he misses an easy one, if the court were in a back yard somewhere, with nobody to see it at all. His "Oh, Gerald!" and "Peach, Bill!" are sincere expressions of admiration, though sometimes the gallery thinks his meaning is "Any shot I can't get is a daisy." He doesn't mean that, but it is true. Anybody who aces Tilden has to do it with a perfect shot.

FRANKLIN P. ADAMS

"Little Miss Poker Face"

Helen Wills was everything that Bill Tilden was not: cool, aloof, expressionless, efficient and consumed with the single idea of being the best woman amateur tennis player in the world. But although she won her first national championship in 1923, at the tender age of 17, she did not achieve her goal world-wide until 1927—and then by a quirk. That was the year glamorous French star Suzanne Lenglen—who a short time before had defeated Miss Wills *(below)*—kept the Queen of England waiting for half an hour at Wimbledon, creating an international incident that made it highly expedient for her to turn professional. Most writers bemoaned the departure of La Lenglen, a witty and uninhibited champion who smoked cigarettes and liked a nip of cognac between sets, more than they hailed the advent of "Queen Helen."

In her methodical manner, Helen won every match she entered from 1927 to the end of the decade, dropping only a single set in the process. Small wonder that Tilden, who occasionally lost, openly despised her.

But even though the writers dubbed her "Little Miss Poker Face," there was a reluctant admiration for the regal Californian, as the contemporary report below indicates.

Helen Wills goes about the business of tennis as calmly as an etcher making a design. Suzanne Lenglen cannot play unless people are watching; the little brown moons under her eyes suggest that she has come to the court without sleep after a night of carnival. Miss Wills, in their third set, was three games ahead of the Frenchwoman. Mlle. Lenglen was obviously tiring. She went to the sidelines and asked for a glass of brandy. Helen Wills lost the match. She would not, matching drink for drink, implore the gods of a strange land.

Masculinity characterizes the Wills game. Whenever she can she practices with a man, because "it is the best training, the men are naturally more strong, though not always so deft."

TIME

Helen Wills, never fast, used a powerful serve to wear out opponents.

143

Man O'War's giant stride ate up 27 feet at every leap, and the jockey's toughest job often was to pace the big horse when he tried to run all out.

"De Mostest Hoss"

The sports writers dubbed him "Big Red," but his groom, Will Harbut, called him "de mostest hoss" and that was a better description of Man O'War. He was an amazing combination of size (1,150 pounds) and speed (five American records in 1920 alone), with an appetite so great that he reportedly was fed with a bit in his mouth to slow down his eating. Man O'War won 20 of his 21 starts in 1919 and 1920; at least once he ran away from the field by 100 lengths, a figure in keeping with the odds in his favor, which three times reached 1 to 100. In the one race he lost—to a horse named, naturally, Upset—he was victimized by a poor start and was gaining rapidly at the finish. Earl Sande, the premier jockey of the decade, rode Man O'War only once and never forgot it. "That day, I knew I was riding the greatest horse ever bred for running," he said. The *New York Tribune* ran the following account of Man O'War's most exciting victory in 1920.

Man O'War proved himself the horse of eternity at Aqueduct yesterday afternoon. Lucky indeed was he who can say he saw Man O'War on July 10, 1920. He saw the greatest race of turf history won by the greatest horse. But for this super-horse, John P. Grier might today be heralded as the equine champion of the age. He ran a race that would have beaten any horse that ever looked through a bridle—except Man O'War. From start to finish, every post of the journey was passed in record time. And until almost the very end it seemed that Grier might win. For the first time in his racing career the sleek chestnut sides of Man O'War felt the cut of the whip. Kummer applied the lash with right good will. And Man O'War, roused to the idea that something vital was at stake, responded as the great horse that he is. He charged at his rival with all the power of his marvellous frame and simply broke the heart of as game a three-year-old as this country will see in many a day. W. J. MACBETH

BOBBY JONES

The King and Queen of Golf

Bobby Jones's feat of winning the world's four major golf tournaments in 1930—the unprecedented "Grand Slam"—concluded an amazing run of success a biographer called Jones's "eight fat years." In that time he won 13 national championships on both sides of the Atlantic. But before then, Jones struggled through "seven lean years," when he failed to win a single big tournament. At the 1921 British Open, he blew up in memorable fashion and shocked the spectators by picking up his ball and quitting cold.

But once he had mastered both his temper and an amazing variety of shots, Jones became a national idol. His adoring public gave him *two* Broadway ticker-tape parades, and the grandest compliment that could be bestowed on six-time women's champion Glenna Collett *(opposite)* was to call her the "Female Bobby Jones."

To celebrate the "Grand Slam," Francis Powers rewrote Grantland Rice's famous passage about the 1924 Notre Dame backfield: "Once again the Four Horsemen of the Apocalypse galloped away together, and their names were Jones, Jones, Jones, Jones." Rice's own tribute, which is excerpted below, was restrained by comparison.

There is no secret connected with Bobby Jones's mastery of the golf world. There are others who have a swing just about as sound, the same determination and the same ability to concentrate. But there is no other who has the all-around combination of these essential elements. This combination happened to meet in one man for the first time in the history of golf.

GRANTLAND RICE

Looking back over Bobby's matches, you may see crisis after crisis where the least slip in nerve or skill or plain fortune would have spelled blue ruin to Bobby's dearest ambition. Yet at every crisis he stood up to the shot with something which I can define only as inevitability and performed what was needed with all the certainty of a natural phenomenon.

O. B. KEELER

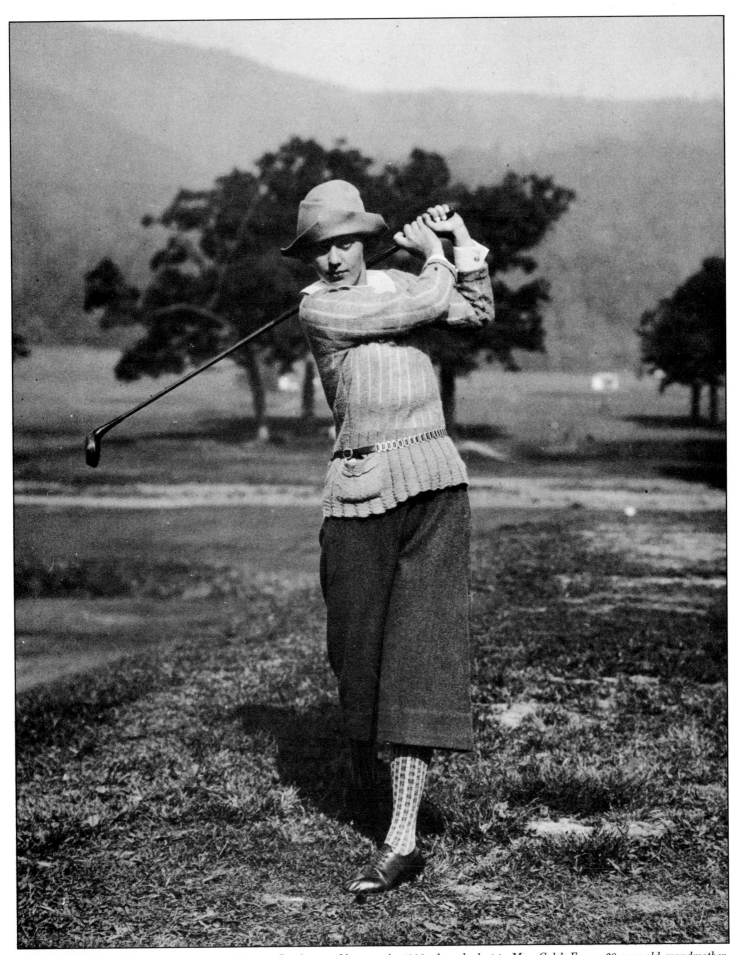

Golf queen Glenna Collett, a fine natural athlete, suffered a notable upset in 1923 when she lost to Mrs. Caleb Fox, a 60-year-old grandmother.

In "The Babe Comes Home," Ruth played a farm boy who made good in the big leagues and fell for a hard-to-get blonde, played by Anna Q. Nilsson.

Stars of Field and Screen

Some of the worst acting ever seen on American movie screens was perpetrated in the '20s by such sports idols as Babe Ruth, Jack Dempsey and Red Grange. Hired by movie makers for the drawing power of their names, they strutted, grimaced, thrashed the villains, kissed the heroines and, not incidentally, showed off their athletic prowess. The critics groaned, but the fans paid to see it.

Jack Dempsey's series of cliff-hangers, titled *Daredevil Jack*, did so well at the box office that he tried a second series, *Fight and Win*, as well as several full-length films; in one of them, *Manhattan Madness*, his actress wife also starred. Dempsey's fight scenes were highly realistic, and for a good reason: the Manassa Mauler never learned how to pull his punches. More than one actor was not acting when he went down before a Dempsey belt.

There were certain problems inherent in the transition from the sports arena to the silver screen. Grange spelled out one of them: "I don't want to play a sheik part. This

---

All lip-rouged like a tight-wire lady, with a voice as sweet as a furnace shaker in action, hands that could not find a place on that whole stage to rest comfortably, a grace of carriage somewhere between John Barrymore and an elephant, Babe Ruth came out yesterday at the Palace.   NEW YORK *WORLD*

---

business of lollygagging around with a girl most of the time is not in my line. I can do all the rough work on the gridiron, but I want to do very little in the parlor."

Another difficulty was finding time for all this extracurricular activity. When Ruth agreed to do a quickie called *The Babe Comes Home*, he acted in the morning in Fort Lee, New Jersey, then dashed across the Hudson River to play ball in the afternoon. One day, after he missed batting practice and showed up with make-up still on his face, Yankee manager Miller Huggins barked the natural question: "What are you, a movie actor or a ballplayer?" If Huggins had been a newspaper reader he would have known; in 1920 Ruth tried his luck at vaudeville and drew the devastating review in the box above.

Bill Tilden whispers sweet nothings to a starlet in one of his movies.

Gene Tunney and suit emerge unmarked in "The Fighting Marine."

Red Grange, perched on a chair back, watches dormitory horseplay in a scene from his one film, a 1926 grid thriller called "One Minute to Play."

Jack Dempsey, whose minimum movie salary was $1,000 a week, registers the proper emotion as he tries to master French in "So This Is Paris."

Prohibition

Cheerful federal agents dump a cache of beer into Lake Michigan.

The Noble Experiment

No person shall, on or after the date when the 18th Amendment to the Constitution of the United States goes into effect, manufacture, sell, barter, transport, import, export, deliver, furnish or possess any intoxicating liquor except as authorized in this act.

TITLE II, SECTION 3, NATIONAL PROHIBITION ACT

The 1920s were scarcely two weeks old when the United States launched on one of the maddest follies of a mad decade. On January 16, the 18th Amendment became the law of the land, making liquor, beer and wine illegal throughout the country. With it came the National Prohibition Act (popularly called the Volstead Act, for its author), by which the Amendment was to be enforced.

President Hoover called the Amendment "a great social and economic experiment, noble in motive." Noble though it may have been, seldom has law been more flagrantly violated. Not only did Americans continue to manufacture, barter and possess alcohol; they drank more of it. Women, to whom the saloon had been off limits, trooped into Prohibition's invention, the speak-easy, where they consumed quantities of Prohibition's new potion, the cocktail. Moonshining, formerly carried on in the hills by country folk for their own convenience, became big business. So did smuggling; hundreds of ships were anchored three miles off the Atlantic Coast in a line from Maine to Florida, dispensing liquor to anyone who chose to come out by rowboat, skiff or speedboat.

Officers of the law conspired with the drinkers to make a travesty of Prohibition. Some of the agents were honest, hardworking men trying to do a thankless job. But Congressman Fiorello H. La Guardia, declaring that it would take a police force of 250,000 to enforce Prohibition in New York City, added sourly that another 200,000 would be required to police the police. In Philadelphia, grafters were said to have pocketed $20 million in three years; in Detroit they hauled in two million dollars a year. In Chicago gangsters held the city in thrall. In San Francisco, a jury trying a Prohibition case was found drinking up the liquor that had been used in court as evidence. In Texas, just a few months after the start of Prohibition, a still turning out 130 gallons of whiskey a day was found operating on the farm of Senator Morris Sheppard, author of the 18th Amendment. In Washington the Prohibition Bureau had the highest turnover of officers of any government agency—some 10,000 men held 3,000 jobs in six years—a fact that elicited from one who remained the rueful comment that the Bureau was running "a training school for bootleggers."

"If you think this country ain't dry," remarked the comedian Will Rogers, "just watch 'em vote; if you think this country ain't wet, just watch 'em drink. You see, when they vote, it's counted, but when they drink, it ain't."

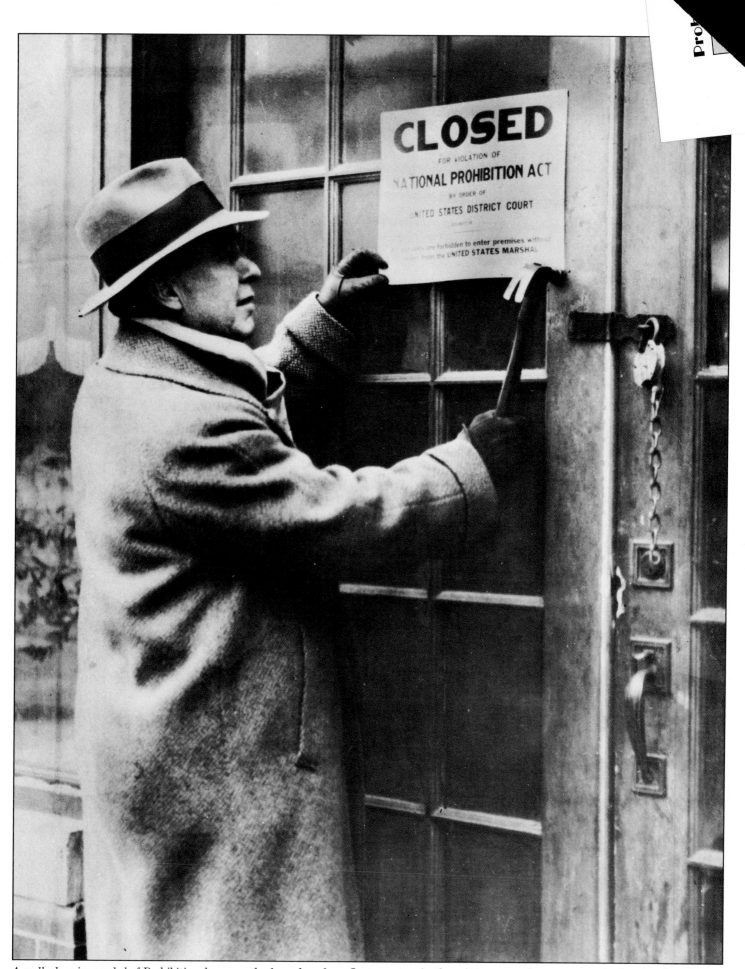

A padlock, grim symbol of Prohibition, hangs on the door of a saloon. Lest anyone miss the point, an agent hammers on a sign bearing the sad news.

"I know who *you* are—*you're* the minister!"

FIRST BOOTLEGGER: "Two suckers got poisoned on my stuff the other day."
SECOND BOOTLEGGER: "Let's not talk shop, Horace."

"The worst part of this business isn't running into the cops but running into your friends while you're in this bum seaman's outfit."

The Talk of the Nation

As the sources of liquor dried up, hard drink became an obsession with Americans. No other topic took up so much space in newspapers, magazines and books—or, needless to say, in jokes. Cartoonists had a field day with such subjects as smuggling, bootlegging, the sale of medical alcohol in drugstores *(upper right)* and just plain drunkenness, which somehow seemed much more noticeable after Prohibition than before.

Perhaps the biggest joke of all was the bootleggers' price list *(below, right)*. The smugglers' ships did indeed bring in brand-name liquor. But the bootleggers rushed the stuff to cutting plants, where it was watered down and put in bottles of appropriate shape, stamps and corks. One man with a bottle labeled Veritable Benedictine D.O.M. noted that the two red wax patches that sealed it had been impressed not by the seal of the original bottler but by a U.S. quarter—complete with the words "In God We Trust."

"Madame, have you any liquor in that trunk?"

"No, young man, and I don't want to buy any either!"

"Tonsilitis!"

For all their undercover hankypanky, many 'leggers openly touted their merchandise. This price list was issued by a New York shop.

The Volstead Market Day

A floppy overcoat (left) hides two tins of booze strapped to a lady's legs (right). The scene was Detroit, destination of many smugglers from Canada.

Before skirts climbed to the knee, a lady could keep a flask in her garter.

Russian boots suddenly became stylish; this picture may explain why.

Getting Around the Law

American ingenuity, which knows no bounds, had a heyday during Prohibition as people sought ways to tote liquor around without getting arrested. One result was the hip flask; others are shown here.

People also hid the stuff in false books and coconut shells, in hot-water bottles strung from their necks and hidden under their clothing, and in garden hose wrapped around their waists, in prams with babies perched on top and in carpenters' aprons with big fat pockets. One man was caught hustling over the International Bridge at Buffalo carrying two boxes of eggs, every one of which had been drained and refilled with liquor. Another tossed some life preservers from a steamship to a friend waiting in a boat in New York Harbor; unhappily he aimed wrong and the whiskey-loaded preservers broke the friend's arm.

A hollow cane was handy in the street and easy to unplug at the table.

The Saloon Goes Underground

The old-time saloon, bugaboo of the temperance enthusiasts, was the first target of Prohibition enforcers. But it sometimes seemed that for every saloon that closed, a half-dozen underground drinking places—or speak-easies—sprang up. By the summer of 1920, six months after Prohibition began, the speak was an established institution—one that the federal agents raided and padlocked in vain, or "protected" for a consideration. By the middle of the decade there were thought to be 100,000 speak-easies in New York City alone. Drinkers said you could get a glass of liquor in any building on 52nd Street between Fifth and Sixth Avenues; the Feds said that 45th Street was the wettest street in the country.

Despite all this, the Drys greeted the demise of the saloon with little cries of pleasure. They sanctimoniously declared that "art, literature, music, learning, entertainment and benevolence all find their finest expression in this saloonless land." They even credited the financial boom of the '20s to Prohibition—although they were notably silent when the boom collapsed in 1929.

Running a speak-easy could net its owner a lot of money. But it took money to make money—one New York proprietor put the cost at $1,370 a month. Of this, $400 was graft to federal Prohibition agents, the police department and the district attorneys. The cop on the beat got another $40 to turn his back whenever beer was delivered. The alternative to making payoffs was to have an elaborate—and expensive—system for concealing the evidence whenever there was a raid. At Manhattan's "21" club there were four alarm buttons at various points in the vestibule (so that if a raider prevented one of them from being pushed, the doorman could reach another). There were also five separate liquor caches, reachable only through secret doors; complicated electric switches opened the doors, and the switches were instantly short-circuited whenever an alarm button was pressed.

Some speak-easies were known for the quality of their food and liquor; others for the personalities of their owners. Perhaps the most famous speak-owner was Texas Guinan (overleaf), a boisterous blonde who presided over a whole series of rowdy places (when one was shut down she simply moved to another). She plied her customers—whom she wowed with a sassy "Hello, sucker!"—with all they could drink but was said never to have touched the stuff herself. Spoofing the law and her customers alike, she made herself a pile of money. Her earnings during one 10-month period totaled $700,000.

At another extreme was Barney Gallant, equally successful, but as urbane as Texas was noisy. His Club Gallant on Washington Square in Greenwich Village was one of the most posh in New York—partly because Barney, unlike Texas, allowed no drunken rowdiness on his premises. In 1925, with mock solemnity, he promulgated a set of rules for nightclub-goers. An excerpt appears below.

Do not get too friendly with the waiter. His name is neither Charlie nor George. Remember the old adage about familiarity breeding contempt.

Do not ask to play the drums. The drum heads are not as tough as many another head. Besides, it has a tendency to disturb the rhythm.

Make no requests of the leader of the orchestra for the songs of the vintage of 1890. Crooning "Sweet Adeline" was all right for your granddad, but times, alas, have changed.

Pinching the cigarette girl's cheek or asking her to dance with you is decidedly out of order. She is there for the sole purpose of dispensing cigars and cigarettes with a smile that will bring profits to the concessionaire.

Examine your bill when the waiter presents it. Remember even they are human beings and are liable to err—intentionally or otherwise.

Please do not offer to escort the cloakroom girl home. Her husband, who is an ex-prizefighter, is there for that purpose.

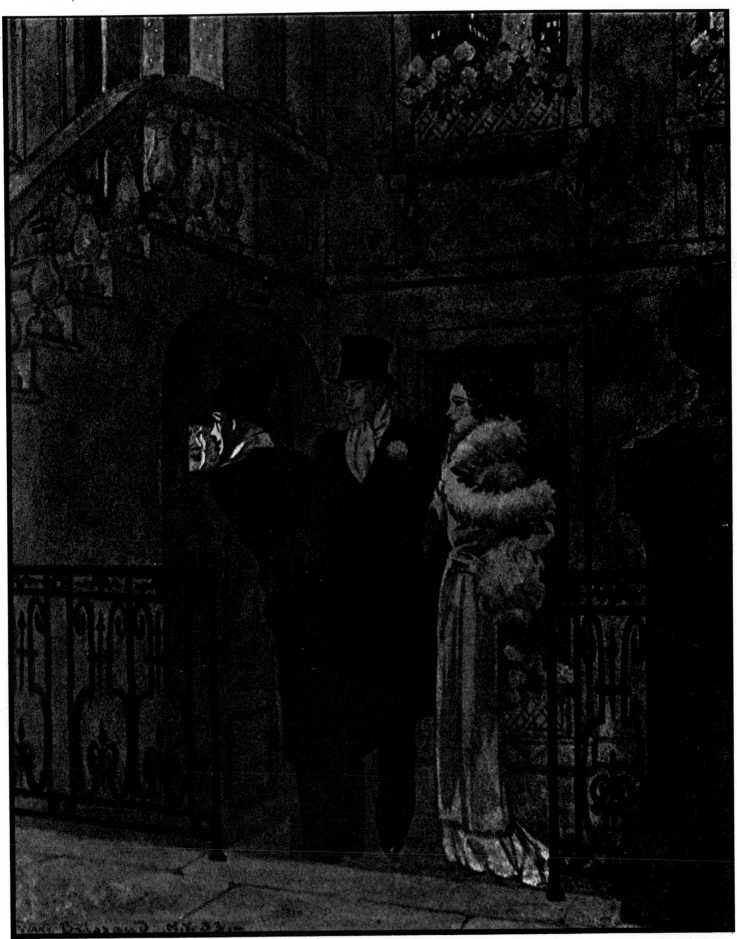

Dressed to the teeth, three New York revelers knock at the peephole of a Midtown brownstone, whose basement has been converted into a speak-easy.

TELEPHONE
EXBROOK 6675   *Menbre*   3117

CHAPEAU ROUGE

Rendezvous - - 2215 Powell St.

MENBRE PLEASE PRESENT CARD   *San Francisco*

WICKERSHAM 2-0977

The **CLUB NEW YORKER**

38 EAST 51ST STREET
Near Park Avenue
NEW YORK CITY

Membership Card

N⁰ 014660

T   64

COTE D'OR

ELDORADO 5-9836   41 EAST 50TH STREET
NEW YORK CITY

NOT TRANSFERABLE

KHinelander 4 { 8038 / 9674   N⁰ 1257

MARLBORO CLUB

Fifteen East Sixty First Street

New York City

CLIFF. 1484   LIQUOR BY THE GLASS

The Corktown Tavern

DANCING, BEER AND WINE

1430 Michigan Avenue   near Trumbull

DIN & RACQUET CAFE INC.   1036 WAYNE STREET   DETROIT

SPEND AN HOUR WITH US 'TWEEN 9 AND DAWN

A CAFE FOR THEATRICAL ARTISTS AND THEIR FRIENDS

SPECIAL COURTESY

TO M_____ AND PARTY

THIS CARD GUARANTEES ABOVE PARTY ACCOMMODATIONS AT ANY HOUR

NO COVER CHARGE   ALWAYS OPEN

Bill Henry

57 EAST 54TH STREET

MUrray hill 2 { 8744 / 8840

LEON & EDDIE'S

Tel. MEdallion 3-8615

LE BASQUE

269 WEST 40TH STREET

Open after 5 p.m.

OPEN DAILY 11 A.M. TO 2 A.M.

Club Maxine

75 E. VERNOR HIGHWAY

PHONE CLIFFORD 0409   DETROIT, MICHIGAN

WHERE EVERY MEAL IS A PLEASANT MEMORY

CEDAR 9461

OLD POLAR BEAR CAFE

FISH, FROG AND CHICKEN DINNERS
SPAGHETTI AND RAVIOLI

COR. STATE ST. AND W. JEFFERSON AVE.   ECORSE, MICH.

HOYLE'S HOMELIKE CLUB

PHONES CLIFFORD

PERROQUET

134 EAST 61st STREET
NEW YORK CITY

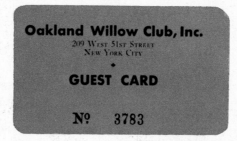

Oakland Willow Club, Inc.

209 WEST 51ST STREET
NEW YORK CITY

GUEST CARD

N⁰ 3783

EPICURE'S HOME
TREE CLUB
119 EAST 55th STREET

EL. 5-9515 9237   New York City

MEMBERSHIP CARD

"The" Club

ADMIT NO. 408

SPONSOR No. 100

4445 Second Boulevard   TErrace 2-9480

THE **5** O'CLOCK **CLUB**

5725 CASS
Trinity

FREE-LUNCH EVERY NOON   EVENING 75c DINNER

Circle 7-8892   2909

MEMBERSHIP CARD

Club Vendome

28 West 56th Street

New York

With the right card a man with a thirst could get into a number of nightclubs. The expensive ones had genuine liquor and excellent food besides.

Texas Guinan, Queen of the Speak-easies, grins as she boards a paddy wagon. Raided repeatedly, she equably flitted from speak to speak.

Do It Yourself Booze

The temperance advocates, who cheered the death of the saloon only to see it replaced by the speak-easy, were in for yet another surprise: certain Americans who had always shied away from the rowdy barroom began to do something they had scarcely done before—drink at home. Half the fun was in making the booze themselves. For six or seven dollars, a portable still could be purchased in almost any hardware store. If the buyer didn't know how to use it, all he had to do was go to the public library, where he could find, on the open shelves, thousands of books, magazines, even government pamphlets, that described in detail the art of distillation. He could then go home and apply his new knowledge in his own kitchen, using for raw materials prunes, apples, bananas, watermelon, potato peelings, oats or barley.

But there were easier ways. It was a simple matter to get alcohol or ingredients that when mixed together would turn to alcohol, and the manufacturers of scores of products were only too happy to oblige. The vintners of California prospered all during Prohibition. Under the tutelage of a former Assistant Attorney General, who steered them through the ins and outs of the Prohibition law, they got out a legal product called Vine-Glo—a grape juice which, when put in the cellar and nursed for 60 days, turned into wine that was 15 per cent alcohol. Wine-growers even expanded their acreage during Prohibition, from

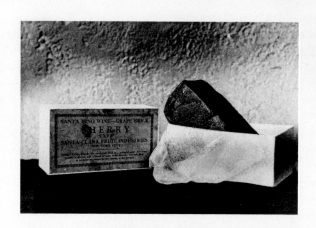

A Brick of Wine

This invention of a New York state vintner, a solid block of grape concentrate about the size of a pound of butter, made a more or less palatable drink when water was added. With it came a circular that solicitously warned the customer what he ought not to do— or else he would have wine, and that would be illegal.

Help for the Patient

Under the Volstead Act, alcohol for medicinal purposes was legal. Doctors prescribed it and druggists dispensed it freely; very soon it was being sold at the rate of a million gallons a year, and the number of "patients" soared. This was one scheme the Prohibition authorities hardly even tried to stop.

97,000 in 1919 to 681,000 in 1926, and in 1929 they got a loan from Uncle Sam to expand still more.

Beer was more of a problem, but the brewers, too, found a way. The Volstead Act allowed the manufacture of a concoction containing half of 1 per cent alcohol, called "near beer" (it had been named, according to a current gag, by a poor judge of distance). Nobody wanted near beer—it was tasteless and had no kick. But before long some smart brewer came up with the idea of halting the process of beer-making before there was any alcohol at all, and selling the half-brewed result, called wort, along with a package of yeast that would convey it the rest of the way. What with one thing and another, there was soon so much

spirituous beverage being manufactured in the nation's basements, bathrooms and (for all anyone knew to the contrary) bedrooms that an anonymous poet was inspired to write in the New York *World:*

> *Mother makes brandy from cherries;*
> *Pop distills whiskey and gin;*
> *Sister sells wine from the grapes on our vine—*
> *Good grief, how the money rolls in!*

Pictured below are some of the other devices Americans turned to in an effort to quench their thirst during Prohibition. With the exception of that illegal can of alcohol *(third from left)* all observed the letter of the law.

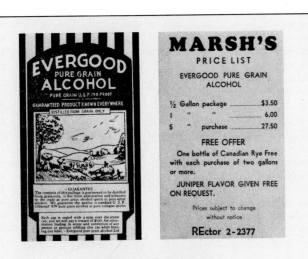

Mix and Serve

"The contents of this package," said the label on the can of moonshine alcohol above, "is guaranteed to be distilled from grain only, is free from adulteration." Maybe it was and maybe not; many such products contained wood alcohol. Either way, the buyer added essence of juniper and got a gallon of gin.

Near Beer

Famous brewers, like Pabst (above), heeded the law by selling nothing but near beer. But hardly anyone drank it straight. Congressman Fiorello H. La Guardia, an ardent Wet, mixed his with alcoholic malt tonic from the drugstore, and triumphantly posed for his picture, pronouncing the result "delicious!"

Enforcing the Unenforceable

The thankless job of trying to make Prohibition work was assigned to 1,550 federal agents, a mere handful of enforcers sprinkled among hundreds of thousands of violators. The task was simply unmanageable. The Feds were expected to cover 18,700 miles of coastline and inland borders—a confusion of coves and uninhabited woodland that were a smuggler's delight. The harried agents also had to scrutinize hundreds of industries that used alcohol in manufacturing products ranging from shaving cream to Diesel engines. They were expected to track down an ever-expanding crop of stills, a Prohibition growth that flourished like garden weeds. They had to watch the highways for the thousands of beer trucks that rumbled from brewer to speak. They had to sleuth out the devious paths of bootleggers, whose ingenuity never flagged.

For all that, the Feds were regarded with contempt by their fellow countrymen, who had put them in business in the first place. They were the butt of endless jokes, and stories of their corruption, their arrogance, their violence and the manner in which they "protected" speaks and 'leggers were told in every drinking place. Sometimes the stories were true. Nevertheless, hundreds of Feds did their job honestly and conscientiously. Agents seized half a million gallons of hard liquor and almost five million gallons of beer in 1921; in 1925 they raised their haul to more than a million gallons of liquor and seven million gallons of beer. Considering what they were up against, this was no small feat.

Here and there a Fed made a name for himself, even in that heyday of the scofflaw, for his daring, his ingenuity or even his charm. Two in particular won a niche in Prohibition's Hall of Fame. They were Izzy Einstein and Moe Smith, a pair of zanies from New York's Lower East Side who endeared themselves to the nation for the imagination and good humor with which they went about their jobs. When some years later Izzy wrote his memoirs (an excerpt appears in the inset at right), he amiably dedicated the book "To the 4,932 persons I arrested, hoping they bear me no grudge for having done my duty." As with many other Prohibition agents, the chief stock in trade of Izzy and Moe were their disguises and the ruses by which they got speak-easy owners—always a wary lot—to tip their hands. To pinch a speak across from Woodlawn Cemetery in New York, Izzy and Moe got themselves up in gravediggers' overalls; to get one in Ithaca they posed as Cornell undergraduates. Another time the roly-poly Izzy (he was 5 feet 5 inches and weighed 225 pounds) rounded up 10 other Feds, fitted them out in football suits and daubed them with mud, and then marched them toward a joint near Van Cortlandt Park in the Bronx, where the patrons were sports fans. "In this regalia," wrote Izzy, "we burst into the place announcing with a whoop that now, with the last game of the season over and won, we could break training. Would any saloonkeeper refuse drinks to a bunch of football players in that state of mind? This fellow didn't anyhow. And he discovered that *his* season was ended too."

Although Izzy and Moe served as Prohibition agents for only five years, the authorities credited them with 20 per cent of all Prohibition cases that came to trial in New York City—a phenomenal score for a mere two agents.

A battered Ford proved useful to a couple of other agents and myself in getting us into places as well as getting us around. We'd drive up to a saloon or speakeasy and rush inside asking for the loan of a fountain pen to write a check with. I'd explain that Lizzie was being sold down the river, and my companion, who was to write the check, would insist that the $65 he was paying was a tough bargain because of the condition of the front tires. And I'd come back at him saying I'd guarantee they were good for another thousand miles at the very least.

At any rate the deal would be closed and I'd accept the check; whereupon all differences of opinion as to the car's worth would be forgotten in the desire for a little drink in honor of Lizzie's new owner. And we'd get it. Likewise the fellow who served it to us.

Two federal agents in plainclothes (top) stand before a factory in Massachusetts. In outlandish disguise (above), they set out to raid a speak.

This Model T, seized in Marfa, Texas, yielded 110 bottles of Mexican hooch—stowed in the spare tire, under the seats and tied to the chassis.

King of the Bootleggers

Among the various and sundry suppliers who helped Americans ease that parched feeling during Prohibition, none was more important—and none profited more handsomely—than the bootlegger.

There were small-time 'leggers and big operators. There were bootleggers whose racket was to swipe alcohol from government warehouses, to which some 50 million gallons of liquor manufactured before the start of Prohibition had been consigned for "safekeeping"; at least 20 million gallons of that total had unaccountably disappeared before Prohibition ended. There were bootleggers who stole alcohol from industrial plants, and others who cooked their own in the family basement. Some smuggled the real thing in from abroad, then cut it down with water, sugar and grain alcohol to make three gallons out of every one they had bought; others used whatever came to hand (if the customer was lucky he survived none the worse). One small bootlegger in Brooklyn was asked what the members of his profession used in making bourbon. "Oh," said the man, "they use sugar, garbage, anything they've got. One shiner I know goes around buying up spoiled potatoes from the farmers. He says they ferment nice and quick. Make an awful smell, though."

Bootlegging began on a small scale; it increased mightily as Prohibition wore on. In 1921 federal agents seized just under 96,000 stills and pieces of distilling equipment from bootleggers; in 1925 they took 173,000; in 1930 the seizures reached 282,000. And those figures, of course, do not include the apparatus of thousands of bootleggers who operated without ever getting caught.

Big-time or small-time, gangster or otherwise, bootleggers often became rich, and jokes about their wealth, such as the *Life* cartoon on this page, were legion. The most dazzling of them all was George Remus, a bookish intellectual who gave up a flourishing law practice in Chicago to take up the hard liquor trade in Cincinnati. Before getting his law degree Remus had been trained as a pharmacist, and he now turned his early learning to useful account by buying up a dozen Ohio, Kentucky and Missouri distilleries that the law had allowed to remain in business for the purpose of making medicinal alcohol. So far he was quite within the law. But then he organized an army of 3,000 employees with trucks and siphons, and bade them steal his own product. If his pure booze later ended up in the cutting plants of Chicago and New York, that was not the fault of George Remus. So profitable was the venture that in less than five years he was worth more than five million dollars.

Remus's style of living could have been copied from the *Life* cartoon. His house was a vast gray castle among a blaze of flowering shrubs, set inside an iron fence and

SUMMER SHACK OF A STRUGGLING YOUNG BOOTLEGGER

George Remus, titan of the bootleggers, peers wistfully out of a prison cell. He served five sentences for various violations of the liquor laws.

This 60-by-20-foot swimming pool of Italian marble was part of the rococo mansion of bootlegger George Remus in Price Hill, suburb of Cincinnati.

Mrs. Remus had her own quarters—a boudoir done in the fashion of Louis XVI.

The entrance hall was filled with statuary and flowers from the garden.

In the dining room Remus often served guests $100 bills under the plates.

graced with every showy luxury imaginable, from a gleaming gold piano to a $125,000 swimming pool. Indoors, no less than out, Remus surrounded himself with sumptuous foliage; his entrance hall was like a Brazilian rain forest. He entertained in a fashion befitting his income and his need for ostentation. For example, he celebrated the installation of the pool with an elaborate party at which all the guests received mementos—Pontiac sedans for the ladies, trinkets from a bankrupt jeweler for the men.

Remus did everything on a big scale, including lawbreaking. In October 1920, federal Prohibition agents bugged his hotel room and in one day's listening heard him paying off 44 persons, among them other Feds, officers of the Internal Revenue Bureau, warehouse guards and local cops. For this and other lapses he paid fines amounting to $11,000 and did five stints in jail—but none of these cramped his style. On one occasion he traveled to the Atlanta penitentiary in a private club car along with 12 accomplices, who were also prison-bound; their every wish was seen to by a private staff of waiters who served a lavish array of food and drink. They chugged out of the Cincinnati station with the cheers of 500 well-wishers ringing in their ears. On arrival, Remus lived nearly as well as he had at home. He ate his meals at the home of the prison chaplain and equipped his cell with maid service—and, his passion, fresh flowers every day.

Meanwhile, back in Cincinnati, his dark-eyed wife, Imogene, kept up appearances, her spirits buoyed by the attentions of one Franklin L. Dodge, who happened to be the Fed who had got Remus thrown into the clink. When after 19 months the prisoner was about to be sprung, Imogene filed for divorce; Remus filed a countersuit, charging that Imogene had conspired with Dodge to get him framed. Neither case ever got to court, for one morning Remus followed his wife on a ride through the city park, caught up and shot her in the stomach. Tried for the shooting, Remus was acquitted on grounds of temporary insanity, and then, a stylist to the end, he repaired to the local jailhouse, where rumor had it he threw a magnificent party for an assortment of friends—and 12 jurors.

MACHINE GUN JACK McGURN

Chief of Capone's gunners, he masterminded a massacre on Valentine's Day in 1929.

WILLIAM KLONDIKE O'DONNELL

He and his brother Myles, "guerrillas of the bootleg war," dared invade Capone's Cicero.

POLACK JOE SALTIS

He was a leader of Chicago's West Side—until he threatened "them damn Sicilians."

LITTLE HYMIE WEISS

"I'll kill you for this," said surly Little Hymie to the photographer who took this picture.

SCARFACE AL CAPONE

His vassals went off on their various assignments crying, "All for Al, and Al for All!"

JOHNNY TORRIO

"I'm getting out," said this heir of Colosimo to Capone after rivals gunned him down.

BIG JIM COLOSIMO

A long-time ruler of brothels and opium dens, he was Chicago's first Prohibition gang chief.

DION O'BANION

Pickpocket and safe-cracker, he made the big time with Torrio, soon bossed the North Side.

GEORGE BUGS MORAN

He was an archrival of Capone—until his gang fell in the Valentine's Day massacre.

Racketeering Comes of Age

Of all the evils to come out of Prohibition, by far the worst was the explosive growth of big-time crime. Gangsters were nothing new (as the Drys were quick to point out); they had flourished long before Prohibition, running saloons, bawdyhouses and gambling joints, and doing dirty work for employers and workers alike in labor disputes. But when the gangsters took over bootlegging—and what better racket to grab?—they opened a chapter in history that made the violence of frontier days look like child's play.

Every city had its gangs and gang leaders. New York had half a dozen, among them two led by thugs named Dutch Schultz and Owney Madden; Philadelphia had its Maxie Hoff; Kansas City had one Solly Weissman; and Detroit, a major entry point for smugglers, had an outfit known as the Purple Gang. But queen of them all was Chicago, a luckless city whose name became a synonym for violence, thuggery and mass murder.

Prohibition was scarcely born before the gangs began to capitalize on it. They organized their minions into alky cookers and rum runners. They bought out hundreds of breweries, and transported the beer in armored trucks across the U.S. highways. They stationed armed men on the borders to hijack other dealers' consignments. They set up cutting plants, where genuine liquor was adulterated. They swooped on the speak-easies, making the owners understand in no uncertain terms whom they had to buy their booze from.

The evil genius of all gangsterdom was Al Capone, first haled to Chicago at 23 by Johnny Torrio, who was at the time boss of the Windy City's underworld. Capone came out from New York, where he had served his apprenticeship on the notorious Five Points ring in Brooklyn. When he arrived in Chicago, a scar-faced rookie carrying the family Bible, he was enrolled as Torrio's lieutenant. In a few years he had sewn up all rackets in the town of Cicero, a suburb west of Chicago.

By the time Torrio abdicated leadership of the rackets and ceded the crown to him in 1925, Capone had an army of 700 men to do his bidding; before the end of the decade he controlled all 10,000 speak-easies in Chicago and was said to be ruling the entire bootlegging business from Canada to Florida. He gave his orders from an armored office that took up a whole floor of Chicago's Hawthorne Hotel, and he rode about in an armored limousine, preceded by one armed car a block ahead of him and followed by another close behind.

He needed the protection. During the racketeers' reign of terror, Chicago suffered upwards of 400 gang murders a year. Rival gangs, named for their leaders—the Aiellos, the Gennas, the O'Banions and several dozen others—vied with the master's own troops in the ingenuity of their murder schemes.

Those murders came to a shocking climax on Valentine's Day in 1929, when Capone sent his men after the O'Banions. Dion O'Banion, besides having a take in the beer racket, had run a flower shop that supplied the

Everybody calls me a racketeer. I call myself a businessman. When I sell liquor, it's bootlegging. When my patrons serve it on a silver tray on Lake Shore Drive, it's hospitality. AL CAPONE

blooms for a market he helped create—felled gangsters were treated to funerals that set records of extravagance in tonnage of flowers, ornate coffins and milling crowds. O'Banion himself had been killed five years before, but his followers, led now by Bugs Moran, were still avenging his death. When Capone had had enough of that, he ordered his henchman Machine Gun Jack McGurn to do the O'Banions in for good, a task that Jack discharged with an imaginativeness that was unusual even in that innovative era. He dispatched a band of his cronies, fitted out in police uniforms, to a garage where seven of O'Banion's men were waiting for a haul of hijacked hooch. The phony cops entered the garage on the pretext that they were making a raid and proceeded to cut down the seven in one sweeping blast of machine-gun fire. Then they spirited themselves off in a waiting Cadillac that the authorities never caught up with in the mid-morning traffic.

Angelo Genna, one of a six-brother Chicago gang, was felled in a rain of Capone-led gunfire. This was his funeral, a model of gangster elegance.

177

Nunnally's
THE CANDY OF THE SOUTH

PERSONALITY
HAVANA FILLED

...ORE

DRINK
Coca-Cola

SMOKE Y-B CIGARS

A Dallas newsstand offers a variety of journals.

A Lively Press

New Vigor in the Public Print

*He was the editor of a tabloid "newspaper" but he loved his children. So he told them
he was a burglar.*

COLLEGE HUMOR, 1927

Their appetites for news whetted by a world war, their leisure augmented by the eight-hour day, their literacy rate climbing, Americans turned hungrily to the printed word. The newspapers gave them a rich and varied diet. From *The New York Times* they got top-notch foreign correspondence. In the New York *World* they could read Franklin P. Adams, Heywood Broun and other superlatively witty columnists. The exposé of evil-doing in high places became the mark of many a good paper: the *St. Louis Post-Dispatch* forced an allegedly corrupt federal judge to resign; the *Indianapolis Times* exposed Indiana's Ku Klux Klan leader as a murderer. Newspaper circulation boomed; the total for the nation was about 25 million when the decade started and about 40 million at its close. The first of the tabloids arrived in 1919, with the most lurid news coverage the country had ever known; their competition shook the old business to its roots.

Magazines, meanwhile, experienced an unprecedented boom. While *The Saturday Evening Post, Collier's,* the *National Geographic,* the *Literary Digest* and other old mass-market giants reached circulation peaks, new magazines began shaking the established order by their candor and iconoclasm. The *American Mercury,* founded in 1924 and edited by curmudgeons Henry L. Mencken *(page 210)* and George Jean Nathan, lambasted Rotarians, Babbitts, Fundamentalists and the rest of what Mencken called the "booboisie." *Time,* the first of the news magazines, started in 1923. The *New Yorker,* launched in 1925, tackled American life with a deft, wicked, penetrating wit. Several old-timers were at the forefront of this vigorous journalism: the *Forum* sought out debates on troubling issues and staid old *Scribner's* was banned in Boston for running Ernest Hemingway's *A Farewell to Arms* as a serial.

All was not highbrow, however; by 1926, Bernarr Macfadden's *True Story Magazine* (founded in 1919) was titillating a readership of nearly two million with tales of love among the shopgirls; a host of competing confession magazines sprang up in its wake.

The magazines poked fun at everything—including other magazines. To the *New Yorker's* condescending proclamation that it was not being published "for the old lady in Dubuque," *Time* commented loftily: "There is no provincialism so blatant as that of the metropolitan who lacks urbanity." In 1929 a series of cartoons in the humorous weekly *Life,* some of which are reproduced here, satirized, with sharp perception, a score of *Life's* competitors.

THE DETECTIVE STORY MAGAZINE

POPULAR MECHANICS

GOOD HOUSEKEEPING

COLLEGE HUMOR

TRUE CONFESSIONS

ATLANTIC MONTHLY

THE COUNTRY GENTLEMAN

THE NATIONAL GEOGRAPHIC

THE NEW YORKER

The Lurid Little Journals

The raffish '20s produced a special kind of newspaper to match the spirit of the times. The tabloids were only half the standard newspaper size, which made them easier to handle on crowded subway trains, especially in New York, where most of them were published. But it was content, rather than size, that really marked them. Racily written, lavishly illustrated, sensationally headlined, the tabloids served up a daily dish of sex and violence that pulled in readers by the hundreds of thousands. The first of these papers, the New York *Daily News*, was launched in June 1919; five years later it had the nation's highest newspaper circulation—about three quarters of a million (by the end of the decade it topped a million). Such success was not allowed to go unchallenged. In June 1924 the New York *Daily Mirror* was started by William Randolph Hearst; three months later Bernarr Macfadden, a physical-culturist and exponent of clean living, gave the masses the most lurid paper of all, the *Evening Graphic*, soon nicknamed the Pornographic.

The tabs introduced Americans to sensationalism on a scale never before known—not only in New York but in other cities where newspapers copied the tabloids' approach, if not always their size. They invented a new headline lexicon ("love nests," "torch murders," "sugar daddies," "heart balm"); they pioneered in the development of the gossip columnist; and they covered the news with unprecedented aggressiveness.

When sensations were lacking, the tabs thought nothing of creating them; in 1926 the *Daily Mirror* resurrected the four-year-old Hall-Mills murder case, nominated a murderer and actually forced the case to a trial before running out of steam *(pages 190-191)*. When dramatic pictures were not available some papers manufactured their own; the *Graphic*'s chief stock in trade was the faked picture, or composograph—a posed photograph with the faces of news figures (and sometimes comic-strip balloons containing dialogue) superimposed on it. At one point the *Graphic*'s heedless news tactics left the paper facing libel suits totaling $12 million; when the agitated business manager asked where the money was coming from, the managing editor replied airily, "Take it out of my salary."

All this was accompanied by pious lip service to the morality of the time. Bible quotations preceded the *Mirror*'s stories on the Hall-Mills love-and-murder scandal and the *Graphic*'s salaciousness was advertised as a blow against prudery. Editorials preached that crime did not pay; it didn't for criminals, but it did for the tabs. The photo of Ruth Snyder on the facing page boosted the *News*'s circulation by one million; the electrocution of anarchists Sacco and Vanzetti was worth an extra 185,000 copies; mail robber Gerald Chapman's hanging increased sales by 110,000. "Some convict was executed at Sing Sing last night," said Macfadden one day to his managing editor. "Run a full-page picture of his face and on it use a two-word headline, two inches high: 'ROASTED ALIVE.' "

Eventually the tabloids would grow more restrained, but during the decade they—and the papers that emulated them—placed an indelible stamp on American journalism.

In the Style of the '20s

The sixteen pages that follow have been made up to resemble the tabloids of the era. The news stories (with minor adaptations) are real and so are the headlines; in some cases the headlines may have come from one paper, the pictures from another. The stories deal with some of the decade's most famous events—famous not necessarily because they were important, but because they lent themselves to the sensationalism that was the hallmark of the tabs. The facing picture, for example, shows the execution of Ruth Snyder, a Long Island housewife who persuaded her lover to help kill her husband; both went to the electric chair in January 1928. To scoop its rivals on the execution, the New York *Daily News* smuggled an out-of-town (and therefore unfamiliar) photographer into the death chamber. His camera was strapped to his leg; at the appropriate moment, he crossed one knee over the other, uncovering the lens, and squeezed a bulb in his pocket to snap the shutter.

★ ★ ★ ★ ★ ★ ★ ★ ★ ★ ★ ★

EXTRA! # THE DAILY TABLOID **EXTRA!**

NEW YORK, N.Y., FRIDAY, JANUARY 13, 1928

DEATH IN THE CHAIR

★ ★ ★ ★ ★ ★ ★ ★ ★ ★

This picture of husband-killer Ruth Snyder at the moment of her electrocution was the most famous tabloid photo of the decade.

OUR AIMEE IS BACK!!

The "Kidnaping" of Aimee

Even in a time of flamboyant personalities, Aimee Semple McPherson was outstanding. A comely, show-biz-minded Hollywood evangelist, Aimee failed to return from a California beach excursion on May 18, 1926; her disappearance created a national sensation. After 37 days she stumbled out of the desert in Arizona, saying she had escaped from kidnapers. Reporters flocked to the scene, among them the *Los Angeles Examiner*'s sob sister, Marjorie Driscoll, who wrote the tearjerker excerpted at right. Then suspicious people began asking questions. Why did Aimee's clothes show no sign of her ordeal? Why hadn't she been parched after her long desert walk? Soon the papers that had whipped up sympathy for Mrs. McPherson were implying that, far from suffering, she had been enjoying a month-long idyll with a boyfriend. The story finally dropped off the front pages, but while it lasted it was an editor's dream.

AIMEE SEMPLE McPHERSON (shown in her robes in insert) gets an uproarious welcome from 30,000 Angelenos, more than turned out to see visiting Presidents Taft or Wilson, as she returns home after her kidnaping. Later, while disciples strewed flowers in her path, Aimee was carried from her special railroad car in a wicker chair laced with roses and carnations.

Aimee's Tears of Joy Greet Beloved Ones

Douglas, Ariz., June 24—Beyond spoken words, beyond anything but inarticulate sobs and an embrace that clung as if it would never let go was the reunion this morning of Aimee Semple Mc-Pherson and her mother, Mrs. Minnie Kennedy. A mother held her girl close to her again; her girl, given up for dead.

They met in the little white room of the Calumet Hospital, a room banked with flowers sent by the people of Douglas. Mrs. Kennedy came, hair running, up the steps of the hospital to the room where Aimee was lying. A privileged few followed her to the threshold and waited in a silence that throbbed with joy and tears.

A PASSIONATE EMBRACE

The tired worn woman in the bed turned a glorified face toward the door. She stretched out her arms. The silken sleeves of the pink dressing gown fell back and showed cruel bruises on her wrists. Straight to these waiting arms went the mother. They held her close, close in a passionate embrace. To those who waited at the door came little broken sobs, inarticulate caresses. For long minutes the two clung to each other. Mrs. McPherson's arm tightened around her mother's neck, quivered. It held fast. There was no sound except broken whispers as mother and daughter wept together.

Roberta and Rolf, Mrs. Mc-Pherson's children, waited eagerly. Roberta's lips trembled a little. Rolf stood straight and steady, his face grave beyond his years. Then Mrs. Kennedy stepped back and Roberta and Rolf ran forward to feel their mother's arms about them again.

When that first sacred moment ended, Mrs. McPherson looked at the men and women who pressed forward to stand about her bed. Her lips quivered, her throat throbbed with a joy that was near to tears. "Oh, you dear people, you dear people," she whispered.

AN EMOTIONAL MOMENT

Mrs. McPherson caught sight of a reporter from the Examiner whom she had known. "Come here," she called. "I want to see you." Her arms were like tense bands of steel, trembling but strong around my shoulders. I could feel the quick shudders that ran through her body, the throbbing of nerve and muscle. "Oh, my dear, aren't you glad for me?" she whispered as her lips clung in a long kiss. "It's so good, so wonderful."

Joy and excitement held Mrs. McPherson up through the meeting, through the gentle questioning of Captain Cline and Ryan. It was not until her tired body could stand no more that she fainted quietly among the flowers and the pretty nurses sent the crowd away.

RECOVERING IN THE HOSPITAL, Aimee is visited by mother and children, Roberta and Rolf.

Evangelist Relives Kidnaping

RE-ENACTING THE KIDNAPING, Aimee demonstrates how (1) her fingers were burned by a cigar wielded by one of her abductors (2) the kidnapers swathed her in blankets (3) she was then tied up and (4) she managed to escape before struggling across the desert to safety.

Struggle to Free Collins

EXPLORER ENTOMBED IN UNDERGROUND PASSAGE

Cave City, Ky., Feb. 2—Floyd Collins is suffering torture almost beyond description. Until I went inside myself I wondered why someone couldn't do something quick, but I found out why.

The passageway is about five feet in diameter. I had to squirm like a snake. Water covers almost every inch of the ground. Every moment it got colder. After going about ninety feet I reached a small compartment, slightly larger than the rest of the channel. I slid down an eight-foot drop and, a moment later, saw Collins.

My flashlight revealed a face on which is written suffering of many long hours, because Collins has been in agony every conscious moment since he was trapped. I saw the purple of his lips, the pallor on his face, and realized that something must be done before long if this man is

SIGHTSEERS gather outside the Kentucky cave in which explorer Floyd Collins lies trapped.

to live. Before I could see his face, however, I was forced to raise a small piece of oil cloth covering it.

The Death of Floyd Collins

Seeking a cavern to attract tourist trade, Floyd Collins, a 30-year-old Kentuckian, went exploring one day in 1925 in the underground honeycomb near Mammoth Cave. Suddenly a boulder shifted, fell across his ankle and trapped him in a narrow passage 126 feet from the surface. A neighbor boy found him there a day later and ran for help. Among the 150 reporters who turned up at the scene was 21-year-old William ("Skeets") Miller of the *Louisville Courier-Journal*. Five times Miller—alone among all the newsmen—descended into the dark tunnel to talk to Collins and to try to help him. But all efforts to rescue the trapped man failed, and while the nation watched in fascination and horror, Collins died of exposure. During the 18 days the story lasted, the cave site became the scene of a fantastic carnival. Mobs of sightseers hampered rescue efforts; Collins' neighbors sold hamburgers for a quarter and rented cots for three dollars a night. The cave was finally sealed off with Collins' body still in it. Miller won a Pulitzer Prize for his reports, which are excerpted here.

"Put it back," he said. "Put it back—the water!"

Then I noticed a small drip-drip-drip from above. Each drop struck Collins' face. The first hours he didn't mind, but the constant dripping almost drove him insane. His brother Homer had taken the oil cloth to him earlier in the day.

NEVER WITHOUT PAIN

Collins' foot, held by a six-ton rock in a natural crevice, is never without pain. I tried to squirm over Collins' body to reach the rock, until he begged me to get off. "It hurts—hurts awful," he said. Collins is lying on his back, resting more on the left side. His two arms are held fast in the crevice beside his body, so that he really is in a natural straight-jacket.

I was followed by Homer Collins, brother of the victim, and Guy Turner. Homer Collins had brought with him some body harness to place around his brother, and we finally succeeded in putting it on him. The prisoner helped by turning as much as possible and finally we were ready to haul on the rope attached to Collins. We pulled as much as we could and estimated we moved the prisoner five inches. All of us were on the point of collapse and after a short time our strength failed.

We couldn't do any more. We left near his head a lantern. The tiny light it throws may bring some bit of consolation.

Sand Cave, Cave City, Ky., Feb. 3—Late this afternoon it was decided that Collins might be rescued by drilling through the side of a hill and tunneling through behind him. The work was started by seven drillers but was halted after a short time. It was feared that the vibration would dislodge huge rocks above Collins and crush him to death.

TOMB SEALING ITSELF

Everett Maddox volunteered today to go back into the dangerous tunnel and bathe the victim's face. Maddox went in at 9:45 o'clock this morning with towel and water. Silently he turned the face of the prisoner as he bathed it. He brushed back the hair from the sunken eyes. As he worked there in the clammy chamber, Maddox read on the face a story of agony and suffering and despair. Earth, using the corpse as bait, is waiting to crush anyone daring enough to venture in. The tomb is sealing itself in collapse. In the opinion of experts, a person going in stands but a small chance to return. Collins' body is in sight but is farther out of reach than ever.

Last Try to Aid Cave Victim

FLOYD COLLINS

RESCUERS prepare to lower a miner into a shaft in the ground, dug in an effort to find a new cavern opening that will give access to Floyd Collins' cave.

BROTHER of the trapped man, Homer Collins watches anxiously at the mouth of the cave, along with the family dog.

PARENTS of Floyd Collins, Mr. and Mrs. Lee Collins (seated at center), attend the funeral of their son.

MRS. HALL ARRESTED 4 YEARS AFTER MURDER

MRS. EDWARD W. HALL   THE REV. EDWARD W. HALL   MRS. JAMES MILLS

The Hall-Mills Murder Case

In 1924, envious of the success of the New York *Daily News*, William Randolph Hearst launched his own tabloid, the New York *Daily Mirror*. Two years later, the *Mirror* made a sensational effort to attract readers by forcing the reopening of the Hall-Mills murder case. In 1922, the Reverend Edward Hall of the Episcopal Church of St. John the Evangelist in New Brunswick, New Jersey, and husband of socialite Frances Hall, had been discovered dead on an abandoned farm; beside his body lay that of his paramour, Mrs. Eleanor Mills. The killer had never been found. *Mirror* reporters collected statements—notably one by the eccentric owner of a nearby farm, Jane Gibson, called "The Pig Woman" because she raised China pigs—implicating the dead pastor's wife, her two brothers and a cousin in the killing. New Jersey officials charged the four with murder. Some 300 reporters, led by a huge battery of *Mirror* newsmen whose stories are excerpted here, filed nine million words during the 18 trial days. Then came a stunning blow for the *Mirror:* a jury acquitted the defendants. The paper's managing editor had challenged Mrs. Hall to sue him for libel (*story at right*). She did. The *Mirror* was forced to make a large out-of-court settlement.

actual scene showing where murdered bodies of Rev Hall + Mrs Mills where found note bloody bags

INVESTIGATORS (top) seek clues at the scene of the crime. Bottom, sightseers gather near murder site (arrow) four years later.

HALL-MILLS TRIAL OPENS

Pig Woman Accuses; Iron Widow Sneers

And be sure your sin will find you out. Numbers 32, 23.

July 16, 1926—Evidence is in the hands of the New Jersey authorities directly accusing Mrs. Frances Stevens Hall and her brother "Crazy Willie" of being at the scene of the Hall-Mills murder the night of the crime. The evidence which may well solve this—"The Classic Crime Mystery of the Century"—has been gathered by DAILY MIRROR investigators. Some of the more important materials have been placed in the hands of Gov. Moore of New Jersey.

And they said to one another, Who hath done this thing? Judges 6, 29.

July 17, 1926—A challenge to Mrs. Hall was issued last night by the editor of the DAILY MIRROR. If the MIRROR's story is untrue the editor can be sued for criminal libel. He invites such action as this telegram shows: "Mr. Timothy Pfeiffer, New York City. This is a challenge to you as Mrs. Hall's legal representative to bring a criminal libel action against me personally if the statements in the DAILY MIRROR accusing Mrs. Hall are not correct. I stand fully responsible for the charges against Mrs. Hall. Philip Payne, Managing Editor."

July 17, 1926—Tell Us WHY, Mrs. Hall

Here are some questions for Mrs. Hall to answer:

Why, Mrs. Hall, did you send your coat to Philadelphia to be dyed, a few days after the murder?

Why did "Crazy Willie" send his clothes to be dyed the night the bodies were found?

Nov. 4, 1926—Mrs. Jane Gibson, heroic witness in the Hall-Mills case, is doomed to lingering death. She has a cancer. When the investigation began she told State Senator Alexander Simpson, dynamic special assistant attorney general: "It is dangerous for me to mix up in this thing again. It may mean that I'll lose the rest of what I have left. But Senator, I'll stick." Yesterday, the woman farmer— the so-called "pig woman"—kept her word. Old Jane Gibson, yes sir, made her way into court. And old Jane Gibson sat there as long as she could. Then she hurried to an anteroom and collapsed.

Nov. 19, 1926—As a doctor and nurse ministered to her lest she die right there, in the white marble courthouse at Somerville, N.J., Mrs. Jane Gibson accused Mrs. Hall and her three kinsmen of murder. She had ridden three hours and a half in an ambulance. Her face was corpse-like, her hands waxen. A relentless cross examination failed to shake her. When the stretcher bearers came for her she looked over in the corner where Mrs. Hall sat and made that charge: "I've told the truth so help me God and you know I've told the truth."

Nov. 19, 1926 — Poker-faced Frances Stevens Hall is still poker-faced. Cold, callous, contemptuous; a sneering self-centered woman, incapable of being moved by the most dramatic and heart-breaking display of courage ever enacted in a courtroom. Sneering, sneering, sneering — sneering and snickering woman listening to another woman, Jane Gibson, accuse her of murder. But her smile wasn't one of mirth. It was a sham.

PIG WOMAN Gibson is shown at her farm four years ago, when the murder was done.

BED-RIDDEN, the dying Pig Woman swears that she saw the defendants at the murder scene.

FOUR ACCUSED OF SLAYING

ON TRIAL are, left to right: Mrs. Hall's brother, "Crazy Willie" Stevens; Mrs. Hall; another brother, Henry Stevens; their cousin, Henry Carpender, prominent Wall Streeter. If found guilty, these scions of wealth face death in the electric chair.

Peaches Says 'I Longed for a Child'

ON THE HONEYMOON, says Peaches, Daddy got dressed up like a sheik, brought along his pet goose, and barked at his bride.

Daddy and Peaches

The saga of Daddy and Peaches, the December-May romance of a 51-year-old New York millionaire and a 15-year-old schoolgirl, wedded in 1926 after a three-month courtship, would probably have gone its ordinary way had it not been for the *New York Evening Graphic*. But when realtor Edward ("Daddy") Browning and plump Frances ("Peaches") Browning split up after a half year of marriage, the *Graphic* joyously moved in. Peaches, anxious to tell all, was signed up for her exclusive story. Then, while she belabored Daddy in one column, the paper enticed Browning into answering in another. The *Graphic* employed its famous composograph (*above*) to give the sad tale a display befitting its moral. When the *Graphic* editors were arrested on a complaint by the Society for the Suppression of Vice, the paper ran this story, too. Why not? It all helped to build up circulation.

WHY I LEFT DADDY BROWNING

By Frances Heenan Browning

My dream of love has turned into a hideous, revolting nightmare. I had to run away. My health, my future and my self-respect were at stake. My nerves were shattered. But can I forget? When I think of the terrible hours I spent—in the night. When I think of the peculiar look in his eye, sometimes! When I think of what happened in his moments of abandon. Anything is better than the horrors of those haunting days and nights.

I am a normal girl with the instincts for love, wifehood and motherhood that every girl has. Mr. Browning did not satisfy those instincts. Mr. Browning declares: "Mrs. Heenan slept in Mrs. Browning's room. To even as much as whisper to my wife, I had to awaken Mrs. Heenan." That is not true. Mother didn't always sleep in the same room. My mother wasn't with us when we went on our honeymoon motor trip. We were quite alone in the hotels where we stopped! I really wish now that my mother had been with me every minute. I would have been a very different girl now.

A FEAR OF CONVULSIONS

I never refused to have a baby. I never said I didn't want one. And Mr. Browning knows that is true! I cried and cried last night when I read his statement saying all sorts of things about me. My mother was afraid I would have another one of those convulsions like I used to have while I was living with him.

There has been a lot of talk about why I married Mr. Brown-

Daddy: 'Peaches Wife in Name Only'

THE BROWNINGS AT HOME shared their love nest with Peaches' Mama. Daddy says Mama was always around and spoiled the fun.

DADDY AND PEACHES kiss for the camera as they celebrate her 16th birthday. Peaches is holding his present—a $10,000 check. Nowadays she says Daddy did it for the publicity but was really stingy.

ing and why Mr. Browning married me. MR. BROWNING MARRIED ME TO PROTECT HIMSELF. Certain police authorities told my mother and me that an investigation was about to be started into Mr. Browning's experiences with little girls. His marriage to me halted that investigation. MY HAPPINESS, MY FUTURE, EVERYTHING I HAD, WAS SACRIFICED ON THE ALTAR OF HIS SELFISHNESS!

Nothing humiliated me more than Mr. Browning's craving for publicity. It is an overwhelming obsession with him. He wanted the newspaper men to know everything about us—what I wore, the color of my nighties, the size of our bed.

A lot of people say I married Mr. Browning for his money. That is absolutely false. Money was the last thing in my mind when I met him. I would have given up every nice dress I ever had to have been spared the

moment of torture when Mr. Browning would come lumbering into our bedroom and growl

Daddy Replies!

Oct. 12, 1926—In an astonishing interview, Edward West Browning, self-anointed "High Priest of the Daddy Cult," stood last night in his pulpit of business and there, amid the ruins of his Temple of Love, revealed to the world through the GRAPHIC the most intimate details of his married life with Peaches Heenan. "I wanted, oh how I longed for a CHILD OF MY OWN," he sobbed out in his heart anguish. Here is his story:

"Peaches did not sleep with me. From the very first night she has always slept with her mother. My marriage was IN NAME only. From our very wedding night Peaches has denied me my rights as a husband. I had hoped to play on the harp of celestial raptures. I thought I

"Woof! Woof!" like a bear in my ear. I was so frightened I went into a sort of swoon.

would be surrounded by the angels of love. Gnomes alone fluttered about. I don't want to say anything unkind, and even now I won't call my mother-in-law names, but she proved to be no dove of peace. I want Peaches back. I want to be a father. Peaches needs me and my care. I won't say she suffers from epilepsy, but she is a victim of something very close to epileptic fits, she rolls her eyes and froths at the mouth. In her story she charges that mine was a strange and weird love, and intimates that I have lost my virility. I am willing to submit to examination by any reputable group of physicians and they will prove that I am as virile and potent as a youth of 20."

Murder to Bare Studio Sins

X MARKS THE SPOT where the body was found. Reconstructing the crime, police theorize that he was shot by a man who stepped from the shadows between the door and the piano (right) as Taylor sat at his desk. A neighbor hearing "an explosion" looked out her window and says she saw a person leave the house, dressed like a man but walking like a woman "with quick little steps."

SENSATION COMING IN TAYLOR CASE

Los Angeles, Feb. 3—All Hollywood is being raked for the killer of William Desmond Taylor; all the queer meeting places of the actors and actresses, directors and assistant directors, cameramen and extras — restaurants, beauty parlors, studios, dens where opium and marihuana and other strange drugs are common, dens where men and women dress in silk kimonos and sit in circles and drink odd drinks— are being visited.

Every one who has come into contact with the slain director, no matter how remotely, is being questioned. Things that may shock the world of moving picture fans are destined to come out of the mystery, it is said. Popular stars, male and female, may be scorched and smirched before the police investigation is over. And all the sins of the cinema colony will be made known. Dope fiends will figure

Scandal in Hollywood

As every editor knew, the surest circulation booster next to murder was a juicy scandal in Hollywood. So when the bullet-pierced body of movie director William Desmond Taylor was found in his study one February morning in 1922, the tabloids were handed a story that had everything. The victim was a classic hero: handsome, brave (he had been a British officer in World War I) and mysterious. Red-hot love letters from big screen names were found hidden in the deceased's bachelor apartment. The suspects were perfection itself: a vanished butler, a beautiful female star, a jealous boyfriend. The papers made the most of all this; the story on these pages, hinting at even more lurid revelations to come, is from the New York *Daily News*. The case was never solved, but its effect was lasting. Hollywood was getting a bad press; that same year comedian "Fatty" Arbuckle was tried for sexual high jinks that resulted in a starlet's death. Concerned film moguls finally hired prim Postmaster General Will Hays to clean up the industry, and wrote "morals clauses" into stars' contracts in an effort to keep their names, once and for all, out of the tabs.

WILLIAM DESMOND TAYLOR

Film Folk to Testify

in the tale before it is all told, and strange effeminate men and peculiarly masculine women.

The police are working now on two theories. One is that a beautiful woman is in the back of the affair—some one of the hundreds of beautiful women of the studio world. Perhaps she was a woman scorned or the sweetheart of another man, perhaps—but there are many motives and the police have not yet decided on any.

The other theory involves an enemy, made in the mysterious past of the dead man which he so well kept from his friends in Hollywood. Detectives piecing together the mosaic of Taylor's life came today upon some colored fragments that do not seem to fit and there are other fragments that are missing.

HIS LIFE LIKE A FILM THRILLER

Pieced together, the life of William Desmond Taylor would make as thrilling a movie serial as was ever filmed. From his earliest years in Ireland until he fell dead on the floor of his study on Wednesday night, Taylor had lived a life of adventure, of many loves and of several fortunes won by hard and exciting work. William Farnum, the famous actor of virile parts, described him last night to a reporter for THE NEWS as "a man's man, and one of the finest and bravest men that ever lived."

Taylor, 50 years old, supposed to be a bachelor, lived in a cosy four-room apartment with his man servant, Harry Peavey. Peavey liked to crochet doilies and scarfs and things. Taylor lived alone with his books and his pictures and with Peavey. Howard Fellows, a likeable young chap, drove the big automobile. Taylor formerly employed a butler, Edward F. Sands, but Sands disappeared several months ago, shortly after Taylor charged him with forgery; efforts to locate him are being continued.

It was a quiet place, this Taylor apartment. There never was a party there, the neighbors say, nor any noise, nor any disturbance. Today, it became known for the first time that Taylor had been divorced ten years ago, that his wife is still living—thought to be somewhere in the East—and that he has a 14-year-old daughter in a private school in Long Island.

REFERS TO MYSTERIOUS "TRAGEDY"

Taylor never told anyone that he had been married. On one occasion he did remark that he had had a "tragedy" in his life. He was reticent, mysterious, a sphinx when it came to discussing his private affairs.

Recently, say his friends, he had been visiting the queer places in Los Angeles, where

MABEL NORMAND, the well known star of Mack Sennett comedies, confers with her lawyer and the District Attorney after Taylor's death. She was a close friend of the murdered director, and, on the last evening of his life, visited Taylor's home for cocktails. Just before she left he gave her a new volume by Sigmund Freud to read, and told her he would phone later to see how she liked it. He never called back; officials estimate that ten minutes after she left, he was dead.

guests are served with marihuana and opium and morphine, where the drugs are wheeled in on tea carts, and strange things happen.

BULLETIN

Los Angeles, Feb. 6—A pale pink nightgown of filmy silk, positively identified as the property of a certain famous movie star whose name has already been mentioned in connection with the death of William Desmond Taylor, murdered movie director, is now in the possession of the police and may play an important part in the solution of the mystery of Taylor's death. The nightgown, previously described to police by servants of the slain director, disappeared from Taylor's apartment on the day after the murder, but was found today after a diligent search by the authorities now investigating the tragedy.

MARY MILES MINTER (right), star of several Charlie Chaplin films, is also known to have been a close friend of Taylor's. Her mother is reported to have warned Taylor to cease his attentions to her.

Valentino Poisoned? BROADWAY HEARS! DOCTORS DENY!

New York, Aug. 23—Rudolph Valentino, the great sheik of the movies, a pale and wasted figure of a man, sighed a little and was still. Rudy died in his sleep. His breath ceased at 12:30.

Millions of women had known and loved him during his short, colorful life. Women had stood out in the rain and the cold and blazing heat to see him. He was dead—and there had been no woman there to say goodbye, no woman to stroke his sleek, black hair, or hold his head, or close his eyes with a kiss. Jean Acker, his first wife, had called up the hospital but she never visited him. Natacha Rambova sent no word. Pola Negri is in Hollywood. She fainted yesterday when she heard the news, it is said.

Even the nurses had gone—and there were only men in the room. He could laugh at that Chicago editorial writer now, the one who had laughed at his slave bracelets and his powder puffs. He was a he-man, dying in the presence of he-man friends.

New York, Aug. 24—There flew along Broadway yesterday sinister reports that Rudolph Valentino came to his death by arsenic poisoning. Circumstantial stories told of both jealousy and revenge as the supposed motives. Immediately upon the heels of the first report Dr. William B. Rawles of Polyclinic Hospital denied formally that Valentino had been poisoned.

New York, Aug. 24—In life Rudolph Valentino drew excited, romance-hungry crowds. In death he draws a mob. Rudy lay in his silver bronze coffin, a $10,000 coffin with an unbreakable glass over his face. The crowd would not be patient and would not wait to see him. They crashed in through a plate glass window, carrying the police with them. They went through it with an angry roar, falling, screaming, hitting out with their fists, stepping on those in their way. Horses trampled some of them. Others fainted. From 75 to 100 were hurt. But nothing could keep them away. There went a girl in her stocking feet, weeping hysterically, soaked to the skin, her new hat a ruin. She was crying: "I must see him! I must see him."

POLICE CHARGE CROWD

As the news spread that Rudy was to lie in state the crowd began to grow. There were the police charging the crowd, the iron hoofs going click-clack, click-clack on the wet cement, and women screamed and laughed and ran out of the way, and then ran back again. The policemen use their fists, grab hats, hurl them away, whirl their horses around. Women faint. Women scream. Women fight to get in.

"Get in line." The crowd was milling everywhere, but finally it got itself into a long, unwieldy, savage and impatient line. A line 10 blocks long. A line of um-

brellas glistening with the rain.

It had been the intention to keep the body on view, but this was changed. Because of the irreverence. Because of the excitement. Because of the rioting and the laughter and the screams. Because some women coming out after the last look at the waxen face of the actor had laughed profanely. It was learned, too, that men were making a business of selling their places in the lines. Ghouls! Making a dollar or two by squeezing in here, moving up, and selling out. Other men were selling umbrellas, sandwiches, rubbers.

All day long letters came into the DAILY MIRROR, letters enclosing poems, letters extolling Rudy. This is just one of them, the letter of an aged woman who signs herself Ruthie Rose Burr:

"So much has been said and written in eulogy of Rudolph Valentino. May I, a three score and ten grandmother, offer my reason I felt for that estimable gentleman. It is a pity that one who so ably supplied to romance-starved women the picturesque and beautiful side of life should be called out. He was the 'wonderful lover' and the finished portrayer of the exquisite fop, and yet giving no impression of effeminacy. I know of no other actor quite so elegant. Until my final curtain I shall miss him."

Mourning the Sheik

On August 23, 1926, the movie actor Rudolph Valentino, 31, died in a Manhattan hospital. In less than five years, the sleek Valentino had established himself as king of the cinema lovers—"catnip to women," H. L. Mencken called him. Valentino's death set off an epidemic of female hysteria. In London a dancer swallowed poison. In New York a housewife drank iodine and shot herself twice before sinking down on a pile of his photographs. Newspapers and press agents fanned the fever. Film flacks hired 20 women to weep at the funeral parlor; they attracted 30,000 unruly mourners who lined up for hours for a one-second glimpse of "The Sheik." When the *New York Evening Graphic* ran a composograph depicting the Great Lover meeting his compatriot Enrico Caruso in heaven, circulation rose by 100,000. The *News* cooked up a fake poison story *(above)*, and the *Daily Mirror* gave away pictures of The Sheik. These two papers ran the liveliest accounts of the event, excerpted here.

Women Trampled at Sheik's Bier

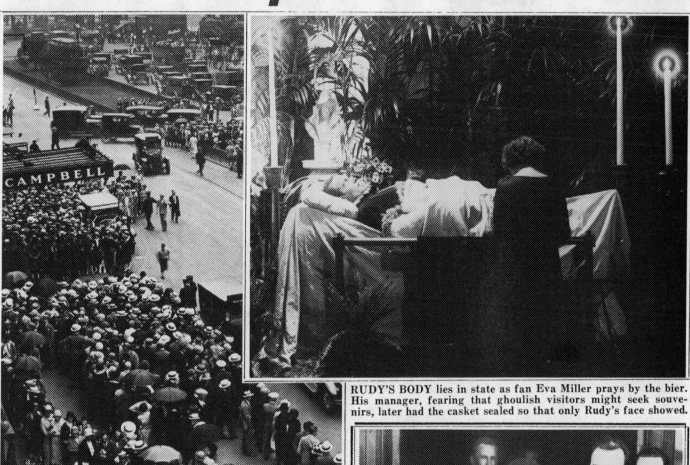

RUDY'S BODY lies in state as fan Eva Miller prays by the bier. His manager, fearing that ghoulish visitors might seek souvenirs, later had the casket sealed so that only Rudy's face showed.

A LAST GLIMPSE of Rudy attracts 100,000 mourners in two days.

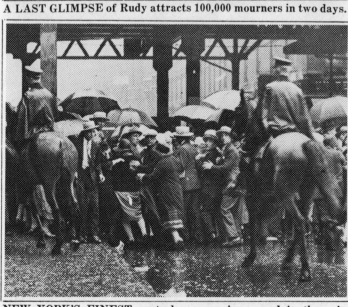

NEW YORK'S FINEST control a sorrowing crowd in the rain.

POLA NEGRI leaves the funeral parlor after saying a farewell to her beloved. Pola said she and Rudy were planning to wed. 197

CONFESS THRILL MURDER OF BOY

"BOBBY" FRANKS, 14

THE SEARCH FOR EVIDENCE takes investigators to Hesseville, Ind., just across the state line from Chicago. After burning Bobby's clothes in the furnace of Loeb's home, the murderers buried his belt-buckle, shoes and jewelry, all non-combustible, in the country. Loeb's father, at far right wearing a gray coat, helped in the search.

The Leopold-Loeb Case

The tabloids had their standard way of handling a big story; when one didn't fit the mold—no matter; they covered it the same way. In 1924 two wealthy Chicago college boys, Nathan Leopold and Richard Loeb, went on trial for the "thrill" murder of 14-year-old Bobby Franks. The great attorney Clarence Darrow, attracted in part by the apparent hopelessness of the case, conducted the defense. In the process he charted new legal grounds based on the psychoanalytic doctrines of Sigmund Freud. Darrow did not deny that Leopold and Loeb had committed the murder; he held that they were so emotionally disturbed that they could not be held responsible for their actions. Although this unorthodox view persuaded the court, it left the newspapers unmoved. Their stories, exemplified by the New York *Daily News* accounts excerpted here, followed standard tabloid techniques. They included a report that Darrow was to receive a million dollars for his labors. Actually, he got only $30,000.

Millionaires' Sons Leopold, Loeb Justify Revolting Crime as Scientific

Chicago, May 30—"We are near a solution of the Robert Franks slaying" was the word from the prosecuting attorney's office as the shadow of the great mystery fell heavily upon Richard Loeb, son of the millionaire vice president of Sears Roebuck and Co., and Nathan Leopold Jr., also the son of a millionaire, an honor student, ornithologist, linguist, radical and a leading member of the so-called Intelligentsia, which has small regard for the laws and ethics of this or any other country.

Chicago, May 31—Nathan Leopold Jr., 19 and Richard Loeb, also 19, today confessed to the murder of Robert Franks.

Chicago, June 1 —"Anything is justifiable in the interests of science," said Nathan Leopold, Jr., one of the murderers of fourteen-year-old Bobby Franks.

"It is no crime to use a human being in the interest of scientific research. It is no more than impaling a beetle on a pin."

"I'll admit we're in Dutch," said Richard Loeb, who helped slay the boy.

The cold-blooded attitude of the young murderers amazes those with whom they have come in contact. Today they went in automobiles, under guard of a squad of detectives, and re-enacted the entire crime.

They drove to the point where the boy was picked up from the street, struck over the head with a padded chisel, smothered in a robe and a cloth thrust into his mouth.

At the swamp the young murderers showed how Loeb had remained in the hired car while Leopold carried the nude body of the boy to a large culvert and thrust it into the opening.

Chicago, June 5—Indictments were voted by the grand jury tonight charging Nathan F. Leopold, Jr. and Richard Loeb with the murder of Robert Franks.

State's Attorney Crowe announced with the departure of the grand jurors that everything had been presented, except only Loeb's confession, which, he said, differed but slightly from Leopold's.

They disagreed, the prosecutor said, on which one evolved the scheme that led to their present plight; which first suggested committing murder for sport, or which was driving the automobile, and as to which actually killed Robert.

Each said the other did the suggesting and the killing, each claiming to have been driving when Robert was slain.

Chicago, June 8—When Leopold and Loeb go on trial shortly, a court room drama unique in criminal history will be staged. The court room itself will become a clinic. There will be revealed, opened, probed and torn to shreds, a new factor in crime —the "campus mind."

Such are the plans of Clarence Darrow. It is said Darrow alone will receive $1 million in excess of his fee if he succeeds in saving the two boys. College students are to be summoned to the witness stand in the startling plan to introduce the jury to the "campus mind" which, it is said, Darrow will claim has become a product of the new theories of ultra-modern college education.

Chicago, Sept. 10—Leopold and Loeb were today sentenced to the penitentiary for life. Leopold showed no sign of emotion. Loeb blinked his eyes.

THE FATEFUL TYPEWRITER on which Leopold wrote to Bobby's father demanding $10,000 was tossed into a lagoon by the criminals. They never got the money; the boy's body was found before it could be delivered. The portable was recovered by a diver.

LEOPOLD AND LOEB (at right) enter Joliet Penitentiary.

A TENSE MOMENT IN COURT

DEFENSE COUNSEL Clarence Darrow discusses a point of law with Loeb (back to camera) and Leopold during the murder trial.

WASHINGTON SIDESHOW
Brief Items from the Nation's Capital

A TRAVELING BUNGALOW, complete with back porch and basement windows, pauses near the Lincoln Memorial en route to Florida. W. M. O'Donnell, shown with family, built it.

ANTI-FLIRT LEADER, Miss Alice Reighly is president of a club whose members say they are tired of being whistled at.

AT WHITE HOUSE, Evangelist Billy Sunday strikes a characteristic pose before meeting President Harding.

KU KLUX FLIERS chat with leader from kockpit before dropping leaflets on kapital.

DO ANGELS SMOKE? These do — and one of them also wears saddle shoes. They were snapped backstage at a college pageant.

The Tabloids, Pro and Con

The tabloids, which thrived on controversy, were themselves the center of a raging debate almost from the day they appeared. Social commentators were concerned by their sensationalism; older newspapers were concerned over the competition. "The tabloids," said a writer in *Forum*, a journal of opinion, "are converting readers into witless gossips, gutter vamps and backyard sheiks. The young are in the greatest danger. If this appetite is not curbed, a tabloid a day will soon be a national drug habit." In June 1926 an organization of New York State newspaper publishers adopted a resolution opposing the publication of tabloids; the little newspapers retorted that what their big brothers really feared was the loss of circulation and advertising. In April 1927 *Forum* opened its pages to the debate. Excerpts from the two articles, which were headed "Are Tabloid Newspapers a Menace?" appear below.

Criticism of the tabloids is the protest of the static against the movie; the drab expressing distaste at the dramatic; the ghostly dead moaning at the ways of the quick. Tabloids were just as inevitable as jazz. They are as truly expressive of modern America as World Series baseball, skyscrapers, radio, the movies, Trudy Ederle, Billy Sunday, taxicabs and beauty contests. They are feared because vital property values and good-will built into the newspapers and the dividends dependent thereon are at stake. Circulation and advertising are the bread and butter of journalism. Advertising pays. Sad to say, advertising has a fickle habit of bestowing its favor upon publications that attract readers. Consideration of those axioms makes understandable the hullabaloo against the tabloids. While the circulation of the tabloids keeps mounting, big newspaper circulation clings by its finger-nails to old levels. Once newspaper men were taught to write in the colorless fashion of a lodge secretary posting up his minutes. The tabloids took that musty tradition by the scruff of its neck and bundled it overboard. They introduced a style of journalism that concerns itself primarily with the drama of life. Tabloids prosper because they are of the people instead of trying to be above the people; because they are in touch with the present instead of trying to relive the past; because they are not only alive but awake.

MARTIN WEYRAUCH, ASSISTANT MANAGING EDITOR, *NEW YORK EVENING GRAPHIC*

The threadbare argument is that tabloid dailies supply what the people want. That has been cited in defense of every stooping to the gutter since modern journalism began. Carried to its logical conclusion it would justify complete obscenity and the rotogravure printing of the indecent pictures which are now suppressed by the police when they are sold by degenerates. We hear that these journals are "breathing new life into journalism." What kind of journalism is thus being brought into being? Here are the results of a study of New York City tabloids from October 11 to October 23, 1926. In the "Daily News," general, foreign and local news received only a little more space than was given to crime and divorce. All the non-criminal life of the great American metropolis was deemed worthy of just eleven more inches of space than the news of marital infelicities. In the sex-dominated "Graphic," divorce received four times as much attention as the local news, while foreign happenings were given less than one-tenth of the space devoted to divorce or to crime. It is a fact that for an intelligent and enlightened electorate the Government must still rely upon the press. If that press conceives that crime is three times as valuable as all the political, social and economic news of the country, how can the Republic hope for political intelligence among the million readers of the "Daily News"? Obviously it cannot.

OSWALD GARRISON VILLARD, EDITOR, *THE NATION*

Notables

Literary figures and friends sit down to poker (key, page 204).

THE THANATOPSIS PLEASUR

AND INSIDE STRAIGHT CLUB

A Nation of Hero Worshipers

The inferior man must find himself superiors, that he may marvel
at his political equality with them.

H. L. MENCKEN

This is a key to the drawing on the preceding spread, which was done by cartoonist Will Cotton in 1929: 1. humorist Dorothy Parker; 2. columnist Franklin P. Adams; 3. banker Henry Wise Miller; 4. socialite Gerald Brooks; 5. publisher Raoul Fleischmann; 6. playwright George S. Kaufman; 7. manufacturer Paul Hyde Bonner; 8. humorist Robert Benchley; 9. columnist Heywood Broun; 10. writer Alexander Woollcott; 11. novelist Alice Duer Miller; 12. comedian Harpo Marx; 13. reporter George Backer; 14. song writer Irving Berlin; 15. editor Harold Ross; 16. Mrs. George S. Kaufman; 17. editor Herbert Bayard Swope; 18. stage star Joyce Barbour; 19. theatrical producer Crosby Gaige.

In the jovial mood of the 1920s, Americans held up for public inspection and applause a new creature. He was the celebrity, the big name in the news, whose most trivial comings and goings were recorded by the press in much the same way that the village eccentric on Main Street is watched by busybodies peering through scrim curtains.

The celebrity might be in any walk of life—politics, adventure, the arts or letters—so long as what he was doing, or how he did it, was sufficiently voguish or offbeat to get the public's attention. He might be a natural curiosity by virtue of his office, like the President, or someone brought to renown by self-promotion, like a stunt man; or he might be someone whose occupation emblazoned his name in lights or in print, like an actor or a writer. Either way, the newspapers and the magazines put his name and his face, his every word and deed before the public eye, in intimate, gossipy fashion.

Some celebrities merely created hoopla; others were at the forefront of the intellectual movement that was bringing American letters of age. The capital of the movement was New York, the Mecca to which aspiring youth of talent flocked like pilgrims on a march. Some of these found acclaim alone; others found it in groups. Among

Robert Benchley

Harold Ross

Alexander Woollcott

Dorothy Parker

George S. Kaufman

the latter, one of the most widely quoted was a coterie known as the Round Table, a brilliant collection of writers and actors who regularly lunched at the Algonquin Hotel on West 44th Street.

The Round Table had an impromptu beginning; its earliest members were three droll youths, Robert Benchley *(page 205)*, Dorothy Parker *(opposite, lower left)* and Robert Sherwood. As fledgling editors at *Vanity Fair*, the magazine that was the darling of the sophisticated set, they shared an office and fell into the habit of lunching together every day. They chose the Algonquin because it was just up the street from their office and because the manager, Frank Case, a dapper hotelier with sweeping eyes and an innkeeper's hospitality, made them welcome.

Case's dining room was already a gathering place for actors and writers, so the trio from *Vanity Fair* were not alone. Friends gathered around them little by little. Before long, without anyone's trying to make it so, their gathering was an institution.

The Round Table's stock in trade was the barb, the blistering insult, delivered coolly to friend and foe alike, and the hero of the moment was the one who provided the last laugh, no matter at whose expense. To be a member one had to be invited; it was not a party to crash. But the membership swelled to some 30, of whom about 10 were generally present at lunch every day. Case, who liked them, treated them to free celery and popovers with their lunch and gave them a round table in the center of the room. Loving puns and existing on insult, the lunchers called themselves the Vicious Circle, but when cartoonist Edmund Duffy caricatured them in the Brooklyn *Eagle* as knights at King Arthur's Round Table, he gave the wits the name by which celebrity-conscious New York came to know them.

They were in many ways an oddly assorted group. There was Alexander Woollcott, the corpulent, owl-eyed arbiter of the theater, which he reviewed for the *Times*, resplendent in scarlet-lined opera cape. There was Franklin P. Adams, urbane and gargoyle-faced, whose "The Conning Tower" was perhaps the New York *World*'s most widely read column; to Adams went some of the credit for launching the younger Round Tablers on the path to celebrity, for he liberally laced his column with their bons mots (always attributed). There was George Kaufman, gloomy and distant, who in collaboration with Marc Connelly and Edna Ferber, also Round Tablers, and a clutch of others, was to write 18 smash comedies for Broadway. There was columnist Heywood Broun, most disheveled of the lot, who called himself "an easy weeper." The only bleeding heart and reformer of the group, Broun spent the decade working to organize the New York Newspaper Guild, a task in which he finally succeeded after some 10 years. And there was Harold Ross, said by Alexander Woollcott to look "like a dishonest Abe Lincoln." A man who could hardly tell a joke himself—when he tried he kept doubling over with laughter, punctuating his sentences with "See?" —Ross founded the brilliantly successful *New Yorker* magazine, which dealt with urbane humor, sophisticated fiction and the best reportage of the era.

When lunch was over on Saturday afternoons, the Round Table men adjourned upstairs, expanded their numbers and changed their name to the Thanatopsis Pleasure and Inside Straight Club, the object of which was to play marathon poker and tell more jokes. The name of the club was itself a joke, of course; it came from a do-gooding ladies' club in Sinclair Lewis' best-selling *Main Street*, where the Thanatopsians, cooed one of its members, "take such an interest in refinement and culture."

Women were not members of the Manhattan Thanatopsis, but they were welcome to kibitz and sometimes to play a hand. The games always went on through the afternoon and evening, sometimes all night, occasionally all weekend. Here as at the Round Table, the humor, much of it ribald, rested on the pun and the insult. "I guess I'll fold up my tens and silently steal away," Alexander Woollcott once said. Adams accused early leavers of having "winner's sleeping sickness" and hangers-on of "loser's insomnia" or "Broun's disease"—named for Heywood, who used one coat pocket for his bank roll, another for his winnings, the better to tell when he broke even.

Poet to an Era

Edna St. Vincent Millay was at once a rarity and a symbol for her time—a rarity because she achieved bestsellers writing poetry, a symbol because of her flippant air and carefree living. As a brand-new Vassar graduate, she arrived in New York "with a perfect passion for earning money," she wrote her mother, "don't care how I earn it." She earned it fast; her poetry so caught the public fancy that before long she was able to write home again that the magazines "just can't seem to go to press without me." Collected in books, her poetry sold in phenomenal quantities of a quarter million.

FIRST FIG

My candle burns at both ends;
*   It will not last the night;*
But ah, my foes, and oh, my friends—
*   It gives a lovely light!*

EEL-GRASS

No matter what I say,
*   All that I really love*
Is the rain that flattens on the bay,
*   And the eel-grass in the cove;*
The jingle-shells that lie and bleach
*   At the tide-line, and the trace*
Of higher tides along the beach:
*   Nothing in this place.*

FEAST

I drank at every vine.
*   The last was like the first.*
I came upon no wine
*   So wonderful as thirst.*

I gnawed at every root.
*   I ate of every plant.*
I came upon no fruit
*   So wonderful as want.*

Feed the grape and bean
*   To the vintner and monger;*
I will lie down lean
*   With my thirst and my hunger.*

The Sage of Baltimore

Henry Louis Mencken was the iconoclast nonpareil in an iconoclastic era, and the most prolific writer in a prolix time. Reporter, editor, critic, essayist, compiler, he aimed a barbed pen at every cranny of American life. His favorite targets were sham and hypocrisy, and as co-editor (with George Jean Nathan) of *The Smart Set* and *The American Mercury*, he made his name lambasting ministers, doctors, lawyers, Southern demagogues, educators, opponents of birth control and lovers of piety, all with Rabelaisian gusto. Warmly admired and hotly denounced, he was known as the "man who hates everything."

Democratic man is quite unable to think of himself as a free individual; he must belong to a group, or shake with fear and loneliness—and the group, of course, must have its leaders. It would be hard to find a country in which such brummagem serene highnesses are revered with more passionate devotion than they get in the United States. The distinction that goes with mere office runs far ahead of the distinction that goes with actual achievement. A Harding is regarded as superior to a Halsted, no doubt because his doings are better understood.

Sin is a dangerous toy in the hands of the virtuous. It should be left to the congenitally sinful, who know when to play with it and when to let it alone. Run a boy through a Presbyterian Sunday-school and you must police him carefully all the rest of his life, for once he slips he is ready for anything.

A boy with superabundant energy flogging him yearns for experiment and adventure. What he gets out of his teachers is mainly the opposite. On the female side they have the instincts of duennas, and on the male side they seldom rise above the level of scoutmasters and Y.M.C.A. secretaries. It would be hard enough for a grown man, with alcohol and cynicism aiding him, to endure such society. To a growing boy it is torture.

Voice of the Minority

Langston Hughes, a versatile black spokesman and stellar figure in the Negro Renaissance of the '20s, was first "discovered" by Vachel Lindsay. Hughes, a busboy in a Washington hotel where Lindsay was dining, placed a sheaf of papers by the great poet's plate, then fled. The next morning Hughes picked up a newspaper—and learned that Lindsay had not only admired his poems, but had admired them in the presence of reporters. Suddenly he was no longer obscure. Some months later publisher Alfred A. Knopf brought out Hughes' first book, *Weary Blues*, from which the excerpts below are taken.

AFRAID

We cry among the skyscrapers
As our ancestors
Cried among the palms in Africa
Because we are alone,
It is night,
And we're afraid.

CABARET

Does a jazz-band ever sob?
They say a jazz-band's gay.
Yet as the vulgar dancers whirled
And the wan night wore away,
One said she heard the jazz-band sob
When the little dawn was grey.

LAMENT FOR DARK PEOPLES

I was a red man one time,
But the white men came.
I was a black man, too,
But the white men came.

They drove me out of the forest.
They took me away from the jungles.
I lost my trees.
I lost my silver moons.

Now they've caged me
In the circus of civilization.
Now I herd with the many—
Caged in the circus of civilization.

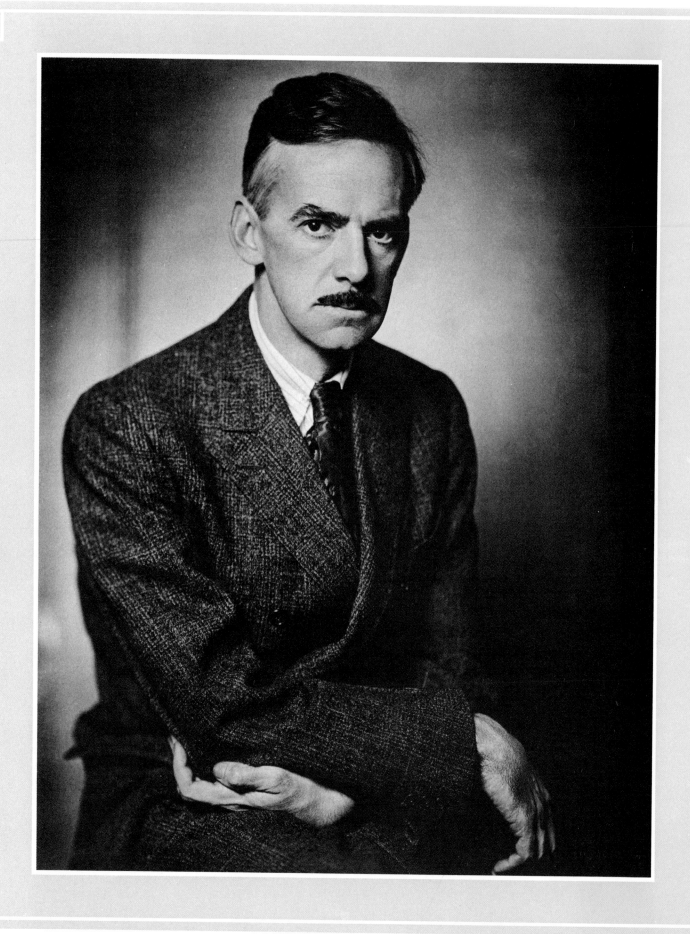

A Melancholy Dramatist

Eugene O'Neill raised American theater out of vaudeville and saccharine sentimentality, and won American drama its first serious notice abroad. This melancholy man, so nervous that he looked left and right when conversing and talked in his sleep of Freud, wrote upwards of 20 plays during this decade alone and earned Pulitzer Prizes for three. His dramas appeared in theaters from Moscow to Buenos Aires. The plays, as somber as their author's face, deal with insanity, murder, suicide and death. The excerpt below is from an article he wrote for the New York *Tribune* in February 1921.

I have been accused of unmitigated gloom. Is this a pessimistic view of life? I do not think so. There is a skin deep optimism and another higher optimism, not skin deep, which is usually confounded with pessimism. To me, the tragic alone has that significant beauty which is truth. It is the meaning of life—and the hope. The noblest is eternally the most tragic. The people who succeed and do not push on to a greater failure are the spiritual middle classers. Their stopping at success is the proof of their compromising insignificance. How pretty their dreams must have been! The man who pursues the mere attainable should be sentenced to get it—and keep it. Let him rest on his laurels and enthrone him in a Morris chair, in which laurels and hero may wither away together. Only through the unattainable does man achieve a hope worth living and dying for—and so attain himself. He with the spiritual guerdon of a hope in hopelessness, is nearest to the stars and the rainbow's foot.

Damn the optimists anyway! They make life so darned hopeless!

A Slashing Novelist

Sinclair Lewis whipped up a maelstrom of controversy and adulation in 1920 with his novel *Main Street*, in which he trained his eagle eye on the shallow culture of provincial middle-class towns. Genteel traditionalists were outraged by the scorn that Lewis heaped upon his countrymen; others found his characters articulating a discontent that they were themselves beginning to feel. In quick succession Lewis published *Babbitt*, *Arrowsmith*, *Elmer Gantry* and *Dodsworth*, which together won their author the first Nobel Prize for Literature ever bestowed on an American. This is an excerpt from *Babbitt*.

Babbitt's virtues as a real-estate broker—as the servant of society in the department of finding homes for families and shops for distributors of food—were steadiness and diligence. Yet his eventual importance to mankind was perhaps lessened by his large and complacent ignorance of all architecture save the types of houses turned out by speculative builders; all landscape gardening save the use of curving roads, grass, and six ordinary shrubs; and all the commonest axioms of economics.

Though he did know the market-price, inch by inch, of certain districts of Zenith, he did not know whether the police force was too large or too small, or whether it was in alliance with gambling and prostitution. He knew the means of fire-proofing buildings and the relation of insurance-rates to fire-proofing, but he did not know how many firemen there were in the city, how they were trained and paid, or how complete their apparatus. He sang eloquently the advantages of proximity of school-buildings to rentable homes, but he did not know —he did not know that it was worth while to know —whether the city schoolrooms were properly heated, lighted, ventilated, furnished; he did not know how the teachers were chosen; and though he chanted "One of the boasts of Zenith is that we pay our teachers adequately," that was because he had read the statement in the "Advocate-Times." Himself, he could not have given the average salary of teachers in Zenith or anywhere else.

Names in the News

It was an era when anyone whose name was in the newspapers was automatically a celebrity. Whether he wanted the publicity or not, whether he was a scientist, cellist, senator or murderer—it didn't make any difference. The press and the radio were talking about him, and in the eyes of the public he had been touched with magic.

People felt they were on a first-name basis with Edward, Prince of Wales, and Queen Marie of Romania (both of whom paid splashy visits to the United States), and everyone everywhere discussed Albert Einstein's absent-mindedness as though he were a neighbor. The man on the street referred casually to the way the great financier Bernard Baruch was playing the stock market or what Paris gowns the Vanderbilt ladies were buying. Evangelists like Billy Sunday and Aimee Semple McPherson, pilots like Eddie Rickenbacker, society playgirls like Peggy Hopkins Joyce, even Freud and advice-to-the-lovelorn columnist Dorothy Dix—all were known quantities, recognizable personalities, friendly faces.

One way for a public figure to make it big was to be —or appear to be—particularly average. Hiram Wesley Evans, the Imperial Wizard of the Ku Klux Klan, declared proudly that he was "the most average man in America," but there were many other men fiercely competing for that distinction. One contender in mid-decade was the President, Calvin Coolidge. In an age that was loud, extravagant and zany, the President was silent, frugal and drab. The son of a Vermont farmer, he seldom spoke in public (though his intimates said he was a maddening chatterbox in private) and he wore an expression that one quipster said had been "weaned on a pickle."

In order to underline just how average he was, Coolidge posed for news photographs showing him pitching hay on his farm (dressed, if one looked closely, in a suit and patent leather shoes). Perhaps Coolidge's appeal was best summarized by the political writer Walter Lippmann who observed that Americans "feel, I think, that they are stern, ascetic and devoted to plain living because they vote for a man who is. Thus we have attained a Puritanism de luxe in which it is possible to praise the classic virtues, while continuing to enjoy all the modern conveniences."

A different sort of popular hero was Jimmy Walker, the mayor of New York City. He was also conspicuously "average" but in a racy, big city way. He wrote lyrics for Tin Pan Alley, never started work before noon, kept show girls on the side, though he was married, and took seven vacations during his first two years in office. But *Outlook* magazine said of him, "Jimmy translated the problems of municipal government, a series of headaches to the average citizen, into simple musical comedy terms."

The prestige of the "average" man, however, took a serious beating in 1925 during the famous "Monkey Trial" in Dayton, Tennessee. The state of Tennessee had passed a law against teaching the theory of evolution in the public schools. (The theory was commonly—and wrongly —expressed by its detractors as holding that "man was descended from a monkey.") When a local teacher, John T. Scopes, was accused of breaking the law, Clarence Darrow, a famous lawyer, an agnostic and a champion of civil liberties, volunteered to defend him. The state was represented by William Jennings Bryan, a Fundamentalist who had been defeated three times as the Democratic candidate for the Presidency. Bryan liked to think he stood for the average man and relished his sobriquet, "The Great Commoner." The high point of the trial came when Darrow cross-examined Bryan about his religious beliefs. Bryan affirmed his literal interpretation of the Bible—that the world was created in 4004 B.C., that Jonah was swallowed by a big fish, that Eve was made out of Adam's rib. Bryan claimed that the purpose of the examination was "to cast ridicule on everybody who believes in the Bible," to which Darrow replied in a withering attack: "We have the purpose of preventing bigots and ignoramuses from controlling the education of the United States."

The Court convicted Scopes and the Tennesseeans applauded Bryan, but much of the world shook with laughter over the spectacle Bryan had made of himself. Bryan's notion that one honest, average man was worth a handful of experts had suffered a devastating blow, and soon after the trial "The Great Commoner" died, a shattered man.

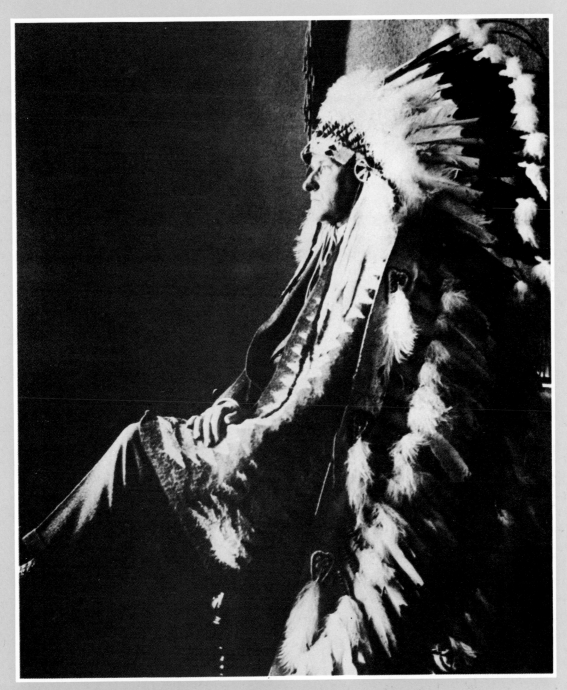

Calvin Coolidge

A man with a flair for publicity, President Coolidge frequently made appearances rigged out in Indian feathers or cowboy clothes. Coolidge succeeded Warren G. Harding in office and sought to free his administration of the scandals that had plagued Harding. A Republican and a conservative, he once said that Government's "greatest duty and opportunity is not to embark on any new ventures."

Richard E. Byrd

Resplendent in his uniform, Byrd rides with New York's official greeter, Grover Whalen, through a storm of ticker tape in 1930, after the explorer's return from a year in Antarctica. While there, Byrd commanded the first flight over the South Pole and had radioed "The New York Times" at the moment he passed over it. The Navy made him a Rear Admiral and Congress struck a medal in his honor.

Marcus Garvey

On his way to a Madison Square Garden rally for the Universal Negro Improvement Association, Negro leader Marcus Garvey wears the fancy uniform he had devised as "Provisional President of Africa." Garvey raised millions of dollars to finance his scheme to help black Americans emigrate to Africa. But in 1923 he was convicted for using the mails illegally and was sentenced to prison.

Will Rogers

Part Cherokee Indian, an Oklahoma cowboy and America's favorite comedian, Will Rogers cracked jokes in his slow drawl on the stage, on the radio and in the movies and wrote a newspaper column. When invited to fly, Rogers referred to his flight uniform as "a one-piece suicide suit" and later remarked, "Here I was thousands of feet up in the air when you can't even get me to ride a tall horse."

Billy Mitchell

A fiery advocate of U.S. air power, Brigadier General Billy Mitchell flew for the Army in World War I. During the '20s he championed an independent air force. When his plea was repeatedly ignored, Mitchell accused his superiors of being "incompetent, criminally negligent and almost treasonable." For this he was court-martialed and suspended on half pay, whereupon he resigned from the Army.

Alfred E. Smith

While running for the Presidency in 1928, Alfred E. Smith stopped off at a Boy Scout camp near New York City and was presented with an outsized version of his campaign symbol, the brown derby. Though Smith, the first Catholic to try for the Presidency, lost to Republican Herbert Hoover, he retained his popularity in New York, where he served four terms as governor between 1919 and 1928.

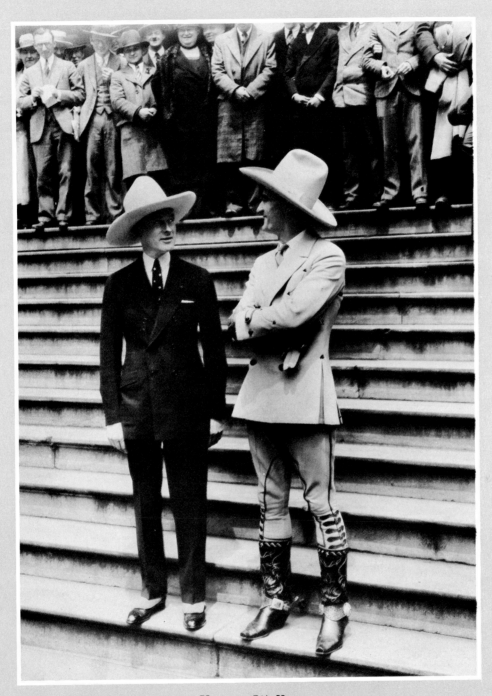

Jimmy Walker

Tiny Jimmy Walker, New York's affable mayor (above, left), dons a ten-gallon hat to greet popular Hollywood cowboy Tom Mix. Costumes were Walker's strong point; he usually changed clothes three times a day. Though he neglected city affairs during his regime, the "New Yorker" commented: "Walker does things of infinitely greater importance. He lives. He is carefree, obviously happy."

William Jennings Bryan

On the afternoon of July 20, 1925, in a Dayton, Tennessee, courtroom, the career of William Jennings Bryan (at left in picture) ended with a whimper. A golden orator, Presidential candidate, and defender of the faith, Bryan had lately turned himself into the Don Quixote of a bygone rural American age, playing the role of Bible expert as a witness against evolution in the Scopes trial. For an hour and a half, sweating and shouting under the baiting of defense counsel Clarence Darrow, he spouted Fundamentalisms and contradicted himself. He left the stand exhausted and discredited.

Clarence Darrow

Social philosopher, agnostic, free spirit, Clarence Darrow (far right) was a man who chose to become involved, who cared and who gave of himself. The great lawyer habitually defended unpopular causes and persons; and his defense of John T. Scopes, undertaken without pay, was wholly in character. So was the fact that after he had savaged Bryan he felt sorry for the lonely old man; Darrow was a tough, clever man, but one with love. In 1922 Edgar Lee Masters wrote about his former law partner: "There were tears for human suffering, or for a glance into the vast futility of life."

Greta Garbo inspired such devotion that her fans were called "Garbomaniacs."

The Glamour of the Films

In an age of celebrities, the most glamorous of all were the movie stars. In the earliest days of the films, producers had tried to keep their actors anonymous lest they become popular and demand huge salaries. But by the '20s the movie makers had come to realize that a big name outdrew a good picture—and was worth big money. Soon a major attraction like Lillian Gish could ask for $400,000 a year.

By 1920 some 35 million Americans were going to the movies at least once a week, mainly to see melodramatic love stories and Westerns; in 1926 the first war films began to appear; and in 1927 gangster pictures started their vogue. The top movie personalities—whether they were cowboys, vamps, flappers, comedians, cops, robbers or swashbucklers—were now receiving about 32 million fan letters a year.

Every aspect of the stars' lives was followed with fascination. The marriage of Mary Pickford to Douglas Fairbanks in 1920 set off nationwide jubilation. When Charlie Chaplin visited England a year later, the British lined the docks to welcome him. Even animal stars were idolized; the dog Rin-Tin-Tin was voted most popular film performer in 1926. Perhaps the most fascinating of all the stars, however, was the publicity-shy Swedish actress Greta Garbo. She was so elusive and standoffish that studio press agents at first complained about how uncooperative she was being. Soon, however, it became clear that her very insistence on privacy was an enormous asset, and the legend of Garbo "The Sphinx" was launched.

Rudolph Valentino, most famous of the screen lovers, gives a sulky pout in his next-to-last role, as Dubrovski in "The Eagle."

The Hollywood Sex Queens

Alla Nazimova invested her life savings to produce "Salome."

Pola Negri, exotic and hot-tempered, dances in "Bella Donna."

Gloria Swanson flirts in "Her Gilded Cage," a 1922 tearjerker.

Ziegfeld Girl Mae Murray was a glittering "Merry Widow."

The Muggers of Moviedom

Cross-eyed Ben Turpin does a take-off on a fellow actor (right).

Erich von Stroheim portrayed a series of Prussian villains.

Lon Chaney wore a huge hump in "The Hunchback of Notre Dame."

Douglas Fairbanks, mustachioed and flashing his well-known smile, makes a daring leap in "The Thief of Bagdad."

The Lovers

Dolores Costello and John Barrymore appeared together in "Sea Beast."

An intense Rudolph Valentino embraces Alla Nazimova.

Janet Gaynor and Charles Farrell starred in "Seventh Heaven," a 1927 film.

Greta Garbo and John Gilbert make love in "Flesh and the Devil," which established her as a star.

Vilma Banky and Ronald Colman act the title roles in "Two Lovers."

The younger set: Douglas Fairbanks Jr. and Joan Crawford.

Forlorn and cold, Charlie Chaplin huddles by his shack in "The Gold Rush."

Harold Lloyd, perched precariously on a clock above the street, flirts with danger in "Safety Last."

Buster Keaton, who never smiled on screen, bathes in a scene from "The Three Ages," in which he was cast as a prehistoric cave man.

Long-distance dancers tango from Santa Monica to Los Angeles.

Fame, Fortune and Folly

Clarence Tillman, 17, local high school student, put 40 sticks of chewing gum in his mouth at one time, sang "Home, Sweet Home," and between verses of the song, drank a gallon of milk.

UNITED PRESS DISPATCH FROM WARSAW, INDIANA

During the '20s Americans were torn by two contrary desires: the urge to be like everyone else, and the urge to be utterly different. For many people, both yearnings were neatly satisfied by the zany fads that swept the country during the decade. By taking up the latest craze, an American could demonstrate that he was a good conformist. On the other hand, by being a little more fad-happy than his neighbors—by becoming the local expert on mah-jongg rules or the best at doing crossword puzzles or the most indefatigable marathon dancer—he could prove that he really was unlike anyone else, unique in his chosen field.

In previous decades, the pace of pop culture had been more measured; fads and habits had changed, but only very gradually. During the '20s, however, the advent of nationwide radio networks and the growing use of syndicated columns helped to disseminate with whirlwind speed news of the most recent parlor game or endurance contest. Simultaneously, publicists perfected ways of focusing the full glare of the mass media on their pet projects.

Crossword puzzles were a prime example. Two young publishers, Richard L. Simon and M. Lincoln Schuster, brought out a collection of the puzzles as their first book. Skillful promoters, Simon and Schuster attached pencils to each volume, devised an ingenious advertising campaign—and watched their profits soar. Suddenly everyone was crazy about crosswords. The Baltimore and Ohio Railroad placed dictionaries on trains for the convenience of puzzlers. College teams competed in tournaments and in New York thousands of fans cheered two crossword finalists in a national contest. The University of Kentucky offered a course in crossword puzzles because, as the dean said, they were "educational, scientific, instructive and mentally stimulative, as well as entertaining." An ingenious minister in Utah cast his sermon into a crossword that was solved by the congregation during the service.

Crosswords were just one of scores of fads that swept the country. Contract bridge, Yo-yo's and roller-skating became popular manias. People competed in rocking-chair derbies, dance marathons and cross-country races. Others hoped to win fleeting fame by becoming the world's champion pea-eater or kisser or talker. A man in Minnesota claimed a world's record after he bobbed up and down in the water 1,843 times, prompting *The Saturday Evening Post* to comment wryly that Americans were "first in war, first in peace, first in tree sitting, gum chewing, peanut pushing and bobbing up and down in water."

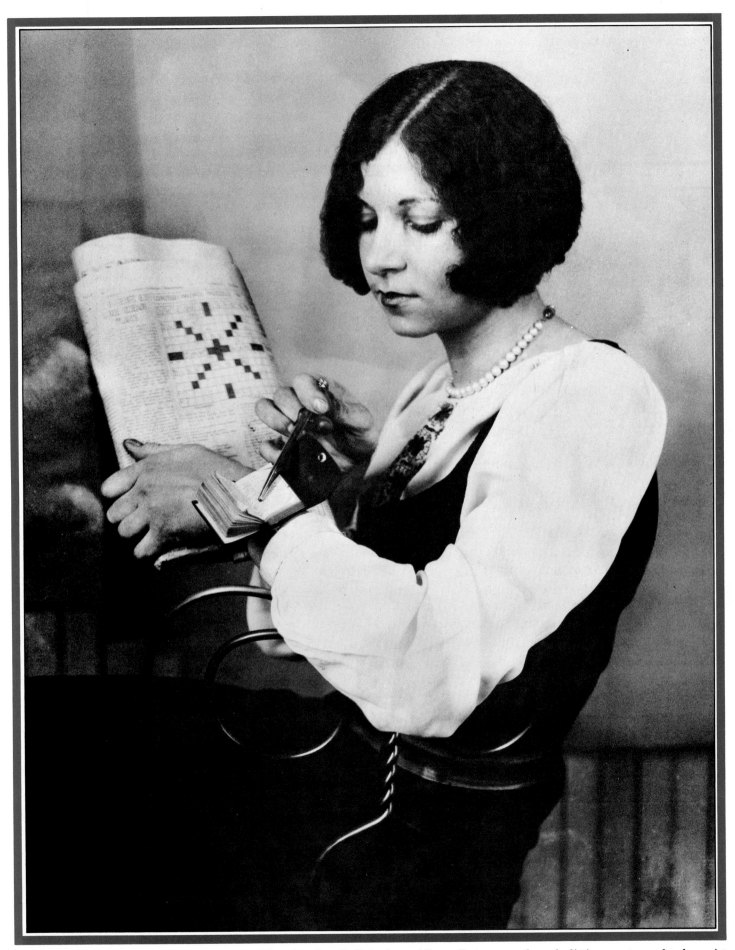

Pursuing a great fad of the era, a girl looks up "Egyptian Sun God" in the world's smallest crossword-puzzle dictionary, strapped to her wrist.

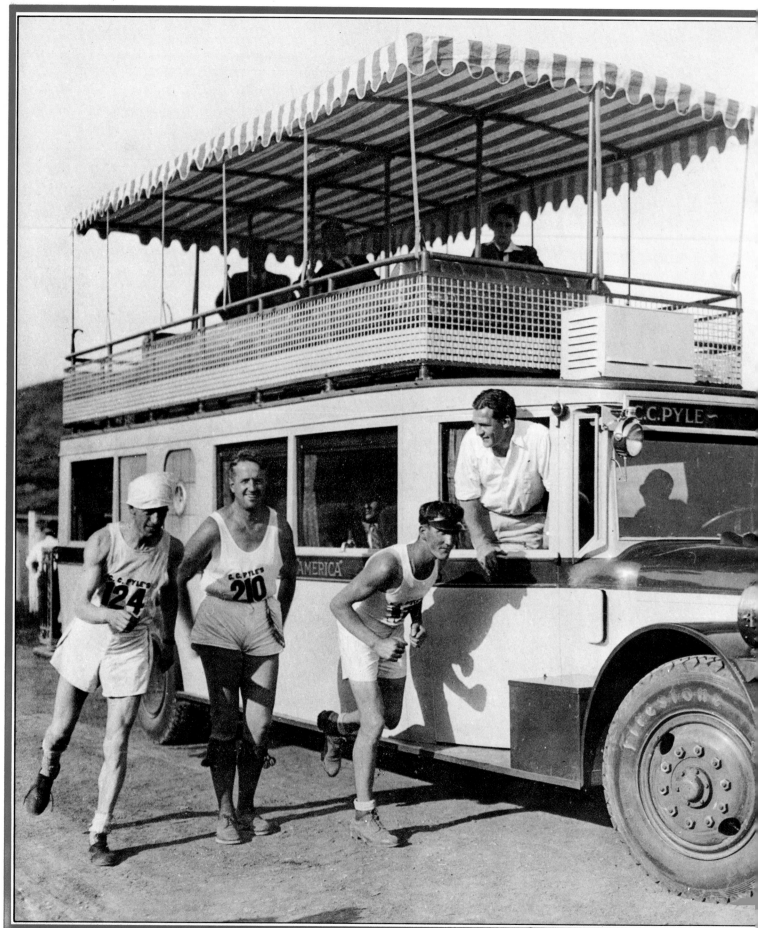

Football star Red Grange exhorts marathon racers as he leans out of "The America," a "land yacht" that housed officials of the Bunion Derby.

Only 2,000 Miles to the Finish

To an era that loved endurance contests of any sort, the crowning achievement of the marathon craze was a 3,400-mile transcontinental race from Los Angeles to New York, which sportswriters quickly dubbed "The Bunion Derby."

When the 241 contestants gathered at the starting line, the race seemed destined to become a glorious moment in history. An official of the contest predicted that the runners would soon be "new heroes for the American boys." The race's promoter, C.C. ("Cash and Carry") Pyle, expected to make a mint. He had charged each runner $100 to enter the race; he hoped to sell millions of programs to eager crowds; manufacturers of shoes, foot ointments and suntan oil had promised to pay Pyle to use their products. In addition, the U.S. No. 66 Highway Association pledged Pyle about $60,000 if he would steer his race over that road, thus bringing fame to the towns along the way. Traveling in a special motor coach, Pyle and a famous aide, the great football player Red Grange, planned to drive ahead of the runners and set up a side show in each town.

That was the plan. But the reality turned out to be something different. On the first day the 241-member cast of runners dwindled to 199. One contestant was bowled over by a hit-and-run motorist (he got up and kept on running). The concessionaire hired to feed the athletes at two dollars a head per day demanded more money and was fired as the Derby crossed the Mojave Desert. The new chef fed the men mulligan stew at every meal, on unwashed plates. Town after town reneged on agreements to pay Pyle. So did the U.S. No. 66 Highway Association. The expected crowds failed to materialize. The side show was a bust. The field of contestants was reduced almost daily as fallen arches and blisters took their toll.

Finally, 84 days after the start of the race (which had been expected to take 65 days), the last 55 runners limped into Madison Square Garden, where only about 4,000 people were awaiting them. After C.C. (now called "Corn and Callous") had paid out $48,500 in prizes, he was in the hole for about $100,000. He said sadly: "There has been a lot of talk about how much these boys suffered. There is not one of them who suffered more than I did."

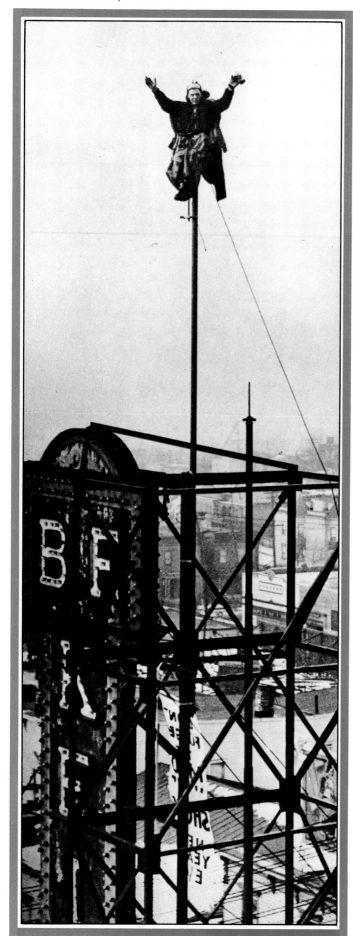

"Shipwreck" Kelly sways above a theater in Union City, New Jersey.

Flagpole Sitting

"The Luckiest Fool Alive," as he called himself, was "Shipwreck" Kelly, the era's most famous flagpole sitter. A former boxer who fought under the name Sailor Kelly, he was knocked out so often that fans started shouting, "The sailor's been shipwrecked again"—thus, his name.

Shipwreck started sitting on flagpoles in 1924 in Hollywood (where else?), where a theater had hired him to draw crowds. Soon he was booked by scores of hotels desiring publicity. Balanced on a small disk equipped with stirrups to keep him from falling off, Kelly took five-minute catnaps every hour and subsisted on liquids hoisted up to him on ropes. In 1929 Kelly put in a total of 145 days on various flagpoles around the country.

All that was lacking in Shipwreck's career was romance —and that came to him one day in Dallas when a hotel elevator girl indignantly slapped a passenger who called Kelly a fool. Kelly, sitting on the hotel's flagpole, asked to meet the 18-year-old girl. She was hoisted up for a chat;

The grit and stamina evidenced by your endurance from July 20th to 30th, a period of 10 days, 10 hours, 10 minutes and 10 seconds atop of the 22 foot pole in the rear of your home shows that the old pioneer spirit of early America is being kept alive by the youth of today. WILLIAM F. BROENING, MAYOR OF BALTIMORE

---

after he came down they were married. Six years later the girl sued for a divorce, charging that his career had come between them. "What's the use of having a husband," she asked the judge, "unless he comes home nights?"

Despite such minor setbacks, Shipwreck's fame continued to grow, and many imitators sprang up—particularly, for some reason, in Baltimore. The Baltimore flagpole madness began when 15-year-old Avon Foreman set up an 18-foot hickory sapling in his back yard and perched on top. Others followed suit, and during one week in 1929 Baltimore had no fewer than 20 pole-sitters (17 boys and 3 girls). The city's proud mayor visited many of the arboreal Baltimoreans and sent the letter excerpted above to young Avon Foreman, who had started it all.

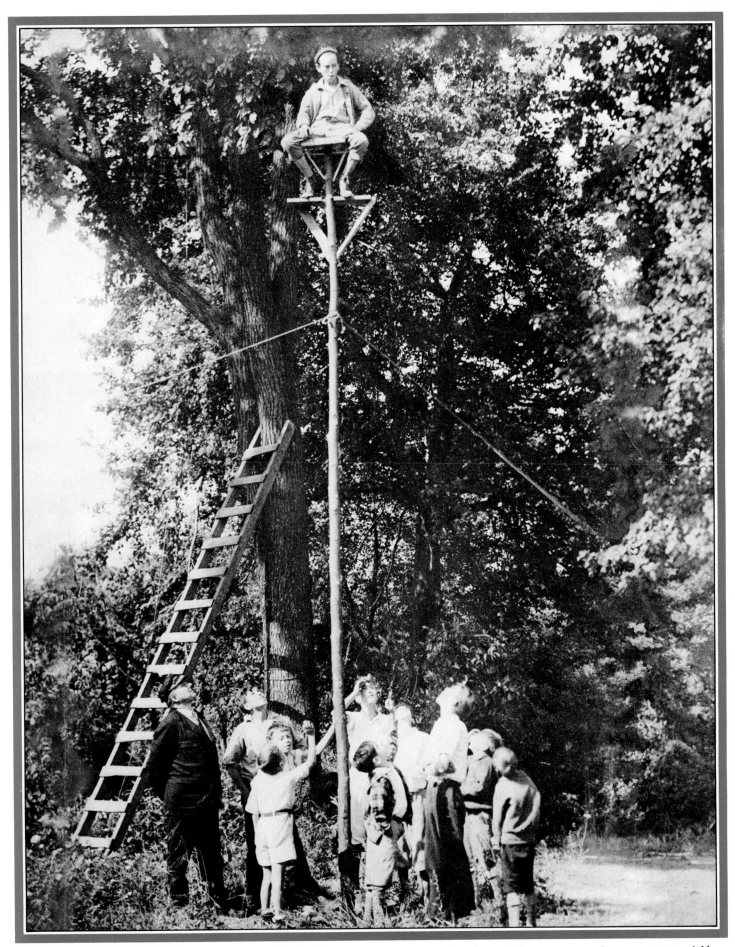

Baltimore's pride, Avon Foreman sits on a platform that he mounted on a pole. During his feat, he received encouragement from some 5,000 neighbors.

Decked out in Oriental finery, a galaxy of film starlets gathers around a mah-jongg table at "the shrine of the Chinese God of Luck" in Los Angeles.

The Mah-Jongg Craze

In 1922 an ancient Chinese game called mah-jongg invaded America. By the following year millions of people, particularly members of ladies' clubs, were shouting "Pung!" and "Chow!" and other bizarre words at one another. Many enthusiasts refused to play without the proper Oriental accessories, and sales of Chinese robes soared.

A sort of combination of dice and dominoes, mah-jongg required a set of 144 tiles, originally manufactured only in China. In 1923 mah-jongg sets outsold radios; the demand was so great that the Chinese ran out of the shinbones of calves, which were used to make the tiles. The beef-packers of Chicago had to ship bones from their slaughterhouses to China so that artisans there could carve them into tiles and then send them back to the United States. American efficiency experts also helped the Chinese set up mah-jongg assembly lines. A good set manufactured in China might sell in the U.S. for as much as $500, although American-made copies fashioned in celluloid could be bought for only a few dollars.

The game's notorious complexities were satirized by Eddie Cantor, who sang in the revue *Kid Boots* a song titled "Since Ma Is Playing Mah Jong." One stanza went:

If you want to play the game I'll tell you what to do,
Buy a silk kimona and begin to raise a queue;
Get yourself a book of rules and study till it's clear,
And you'll know the game when you've got whiskers down to here.

As the song implies, the rules of play, also made in China, were inscrutable and subject to constant change. During the decade more than 20 rule books were issued, often wildly at variance with one another. On the West Coast, where the game was particularly popular, the Seattle *Daily Times* printed a mah-jongg column in which new rule interpretations were offered. One rule book complained that the game was being ruined by "expert" instructors who made up regulations as they went along. "Even the Chinese in America are not without reproach," the book said, "for certain of them have posed as professional teachers although their acquaintance with the game has been of shorter duration than that of many Americans."

A Dance to Exhaustion

"Of all the crazy competitions ever invented," the New York *World* remarked in 1923, "the dancing marathon wins by a considerable margin of lunacy." The object of these strange contests was to see which couple could outdance—or outlive—all the others. All across the country men and women staggered in near-exhaustion to the tune of fox trots played by Victrolas or seedy little bands.

The dancers sometimes competed for prizes of as much as several thousand dollars. The spectators came to see the antics of the performers. In order to keep their partners awake, dancers would kick and punch them and offer them smelling salts and ice packs. Unprincipled contestants would slip their rivals drinks containing sleeping pills or laxatives. After seven or eight days of painful plodding (in 1930 a Chicago marathon went on for 119 days) dancers would often start acting peculiarly. Girls would come to hate their partners so much they would scream

---

There is nothing inspiring in seeing an extremely tired pretty girl in a worn bathrobe, dingy white stockings in rolls about scuffing felt slippers, her eyes half shut, her arms hung over her partner's shoulders, drag aching feet that seemed glued to the floor in one short, agonizing step after another. NEW YORK *WORLD*, 1923

---

when they saw them. One man in New York suffered from delusions that someone was picking his pocket; he was disqualified when he ran off the floor and down the street chasing an imaginary culprit.

One of the few contestants who never seemed to suffer from mental problems or aching feet was Mary "Hercules" Promitis of Pittsburgh. She never divulged how she retained her sanity, but she did reveal how she kept her feet in shape. Learning that bare-fisted prize fighters often pickled their hands, Hercules soaked her feet in brine and vinegar for three weeks before a 1928 Madison Square Garden marathon. So successful was the method that when the New York health commissioner finally ended the dance, after three weeks, Mary was still feeling no pain.

Starting pistol ready, a promoter prepares to launch a marathon in Dallas. The tidiness of the contestants demonstrates that the event has not yet begun.

During the 15-minute recess that marathons gave contestants after every hour, a bedraggled girl has her feet massaged and her pulse checked.

Here She Comes – Miss America!

In 1921 the first contest to select a Miss America was held in Atlantic City and it epitomized the hokum of the '20s. First of all, it was a money-making scheme devised by the town fathers and local newsmen to promote the resort; the pageant was staged immediately after Labor Day as an effort to keep tourists in town and the hotels full. Secondly, the competition became immensely popular because it promised to take an ordinary, good-looking girl and turn her into a celebrity; Americans everywhere were pleased by the notion that through the contest some Little Miss Nobody could achieve instant distinction and become an idolized Somebody.

The first contest was a modest affair. Only eight girls entered and most of the public attention centered on the judge, or "King Neptune," who was Hudson Maxim of the armaments-inventing Maxims. By 1924, however, 83 girls were seeking the first prize, and by 1927 the festivities had become an exhausting, week-long bore. On the first day the girls (who then represented cities rather than states) endured a long official greeting and lunch with the local Rotary Club. On the second day they went to a rehearsal in the morning, viewed a Baby and Juvenile Parade in the afternoon (a prize was given for the cutest child aged two to six) and, in the evening, attended a ball. On the third morning the girls participated in a bathing-suit contest —attired, by official decree, in Annette Kellerman bathing suits. That afternoon they rode in decorated floats, this time donning the mandatory "Fancy Silk Celanese Violet Ray Bathing Suit." In the evening they competed for the title of "Most Beautiful Girl in Evening Gown" (no manufacturer specified). On the fourth day Miss America was finally selected from among the exhausted contestants. In the afternoon there was another dreary parade and that evening yet another event—the Coronation.

The contestants were so harassed and exploited that after 1924 Trenton, New Jersey, refused to send any more candidates. The Trenton *Evening Times*, which had sponsored the previous year's contestant, wrote the director of the contest an indignant letter complaining of the treatment she had received: "We had assured 'Miss Trenton' a week in Atlantic City that would include abundant time to enjoy the bathing, the promenading advantages of the Boardwalk and other pleasant phases of social life. She was never given time during the progress of the tournament to take a dip in the ocean or a stroll on the Boardwalk. The program laid out by your committee not only seriously taxed the physical strength of 'Miss Trenton' but there was also manifested no apparent consideration for the natural modesty of the young women who participated." The *Times* was not alone in its concern for the morals of girls who paraded in swimsuits in front of men, as is demonstrated by the articles excerpted below.

Charging that the Atlantic City bathing beauty parade exposed the young women participants to serious perils, the Directors of the Young Women's Christian Association adopted a resolution today condemning the annual fete. "The board has felt for a long time that such contests are harmful in every way," the letter says. "The notoriety is unsettling. The girls are exposed to grave dangers from unscrupulous persons, and the shocking costumes which such contests encourage certainly call for protests from organizations interested in girls' welfare."

ATLANTIC CITY PRESS, APRIL 19, 1924

Nowadays some of the resorts seem to have adopted a form of advertising which combines a maximum amount of sophistication with a minimum amount of brains and imagination. We can think of nothing better designed to develop a false point of view in the minds of the youthful contestants for these beauty prizes than the notoriety which is given to them in the press and film. These contests lack the wholesomeness of almost any kind of athletic contest, for victory is given for something which has no relation to achievement or skill.

THE OUTLOOK, SEPTEMBER 10, 1924

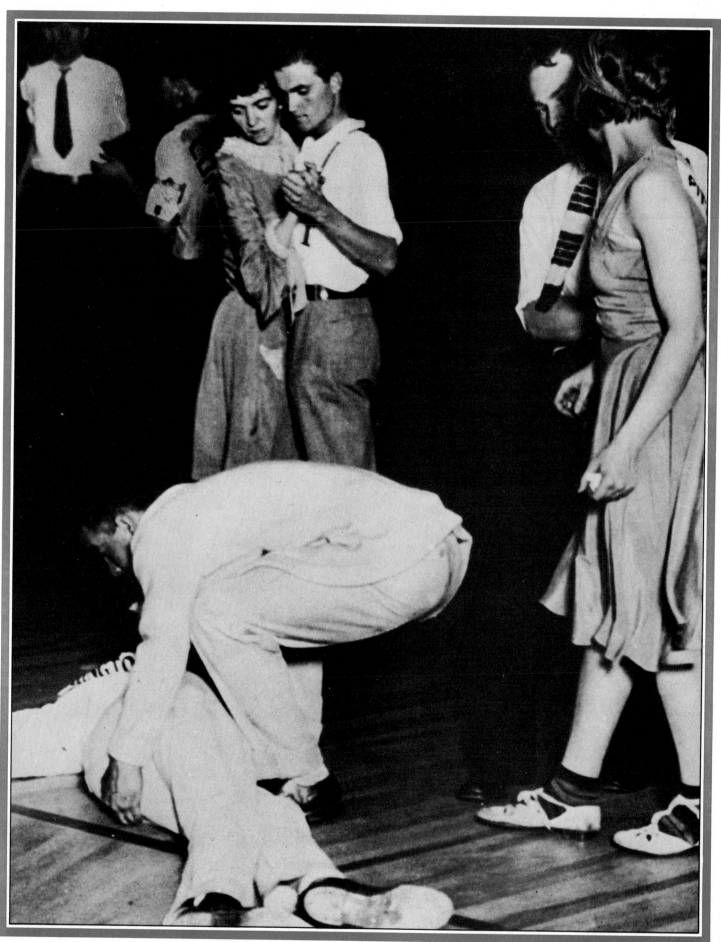

An orderly administers to a dancer who has collapsed at a marathon in Los Angeles. Many contestants died of heart failure during marathons.

On the Road

A weekend traffic jam backs up a long line of cars on a Michigan road

Wearing the banners of their cities, Miss America contestants—including the ultimate winner, Miss Philadelphia—line up for review in 1924.

King Neptune presents Ruth Malcolmson, 1924 victor, with a crown and trophy. Ruth measured 34-25-34 and weighed a hefty 137 pounds.

The Four-wheeled American Dream

"Why on earth do you need to study what's changing this country?" asked a lifelong resident and shrewd observer of the Middle West. "I can tell you what's happening in just four letters: A-U-T-O."

MIDDLETOWN BY ROBERT AND HELEN LYND, 1929

In the '20s the automobile created the greatest revolution in American life ever caused by a single device. It changed courtship habits and family ways, allowed more workers to live in green country and commute to city jobs and ended the farmer's dreary isolation. It decentralized cities and created huge, sprawling suburbs, took families off for Sunday outings and decreased church attendance. It gave hard-working Americans an escape to fun and new sights, reasserted their independence and saddled them with debt (by 1925, three of every four cars were bought on the installment plan).

It transformed the country's economy. With 23 million cars registered (in the late '20s), the automobile became America's biggest industry—its single largest customer for steel, lead, rubber, nickel and gasoline, as well as its most desired commodity. Rent and insurance excepted, one dollar of every five that consumers spent went for autos and their upkeep.

But the auto was more than a practical means; it struck roots deep in the national psyche, became part of the American dream. "To George F. Babbitt," wrote Sinclair Lewis in 1922, "as to most prosperous citizens of Zenith, his motor car was poetry and tragedy, love and heroism."

The manual laborer on the south side of the tracks felt the same way. Asked what the men were working for, a trade union official replied: "Twenty-five percent are fighting to keep their heads above water; 10% want to own their own homes; 65% are working to pay for cars." A working-class wife, interviewed by sociologists Robert and Helen Lynd for their book, *Middletown*, commented: "I'd rather go without food than give up the car."

Meanwhile, the object of this adoration grew even more desirable, acquiring hydraulic brakes in 1920, balloon tires in 1922. It became more attractive, with sweeping, rakish fenders and fast-drying colorful lacquers, and more comfortable, too. In 1919 some 90 per cent of auto bodies were open; 10 years later 90 per cent were closed. While the mass producers reached for new records (5.3 million cars in 1929), a few companies were providing the rich and near-rich with individuality and distinction. "In the city of Zenith," wrote Lewis, "a family's motor indicated its social rank and where Babbitt as a boy had aspired to the Presidency, his son Ted aspired to a Packard Twin Six."

It was the Golden Age of the automobile. Cars were never handsomer—and they were making changes in the way Americans lived; changes that would never be reversed.

Two for the Sports Set

It is usual for catalogues to deal in superlatives.

But the Stutz motor car has no need of superlatives. Allow us to say simply this:

"It is our conviction that this new Stutz is the greatest car ever built."

STUTZ BROCHURE

The Stutz Motor Car Company led a double life. It produced some of the most luxurious automobiles in the U.S.; it also built some of the world's toughest competition cars. Both types reflected a Stutz passion for technical excellence. The sporty custom-built Torpedo illustrated here had a long list of safety features including hydraulic brakes, all-round safety glass, and a "Noback" device that prevented the car from rolling back on hills ("the great army of women drivers, particularly, will welcome this innovation").

The Pierce-Arrow two-passenger runabout boasted a powerful six-cylinder dual-valve engine and a low-slung body that was not only an esthetic delight but a contribution to the car's roadability. ("Graceful lines," said the company's catalogue, "are as essential as adequate power.") This custom-built machine came equipped with a number of interesting extras, including a power-driven air pump for inflating the tires, an inspection lamp and a grease gun for do-it-yourself lubrication. It cost about $7,000.

1921 Pierce-Arrow Two-Passenger Runabout

Movie starlet Ethel Jackson achieves the height of glamor
by being photographed in a Lincoln Coaching Brougham.

The swooping, dipping lines and the side lamps of this Lincoln reflect an effort to recapture the elegance of the old horse-
drawn carriage. "The picturesque smartness of the coach,"
said the company's literature hopefully, "always alluringly
attractive, lives anew in the motor car design." Maybe it did;
certainly it was achieved at great cost and difficulty. Lincoln
bodies were made in the exclusive carriage shops of Brunn,
Dietrich, Le Baron and others. The brougham shown here
was custom-crafted by Judkins, one car at a time; the cost
was about $8,500. Lincolns were not remodeled every year; "it
would be unjust in the extreme," said the brochure, "to subject
Lincoln owners to that artificial and wasteful depreciation."

A Fond Return to Coaching Days

Emblematic of the days when the gentry of England and America found enjoyment in travel behind prancing horses, this coaching brougham commands immediate interest. Old World picturesqueness lives anew. English coaching colors enliven the exterior. The interior is a true reproduction of the early Concord coaches.

LINCOLN BROCHURE

1927 Lincoln Coaching Brougham

A Luxury Phaeton Designed Nature's Way

In the automotive world, it is not enough that cars be colorful. They should

be colored as nature paints. The deep green of the forest is peaceful, cheerful, refreshing.

It invites to relaxation, to whole-souled enjoyment of the hour.

CADILLAC BROCHURE

In the 1920s, Cadillac, the luxury division of General Motors, produced not only limousines and family sedans, but lively open cars like the model shown here. The Sport Phaeton boasted all the mechanical advances for which Cadillac was known. In addition, it possessed a few special features. It had not one folding windshield, but two; the second was installed in front of the second seat. The sales literature also called proud attention to the car's searchlight, "mounted on a nickeled stanchion on the right running board." In

1927, when this car was introduced, the company's brochures fell prey to the intoxicating influence of Nature, as indicated above. This led to some of the lushest sales pitches of the decade, delivered in hushed, cathedral-like prose: "Forms crumble. Motion finally comes to rest. Sound sinks to silence. Color alone abides. Here, in a rose resplendent in June sunlight; in the lavender shadows on January snows; in the adamantine heart of a gem buried deep in the core of earth—Nature hangs her earth with rich tapestries."

1928 Cadillac Four-Passenger Sport Phaeton

Hollywood's Harry Carey, a straight-shooter famed for cowboy roles, owned a custom-built Phaeton.

Elegance without Waste

Packard luxury is mental no less than physical. The feeling of complete security, born of easy control, safe steering and effortless braking, is a luxury. So is the assurance of brilliant and trustworthy performance—and pride in a universally acclaimed, unchanging beauty of design and color. Nothing the world can offer is finer. That knowledge, perhaps, is the greatest luxury of all.

PACKARD ADVERTISEMENT

Although the Packard company heavily emphasized luxury in its advertising (above), and in its brochure insisted that "roomy convenience is the keynote of this car," the 6=40 Runabout actually was a tight fit for four. While the two passengers up front lounged comfortably on handcrushed leather upholstery, amidst deep pile rugs and burled walnut panelling, the other two were crammed into the rumble seat, exposed to all weather. The engineering was excellent; the car had a magnificent engine and the seats themselves had "first been studied with a scientific knowledge of how muscles may best be relaxed." The luggage space, however, seemed more like a sudden afterthought than a well-planned (or even useful) facility. By utilizing the narrow space between the front and rumble seats, the 6=40 offered what Packard called a "luggage well" on top, with locking lids. Hollowed into the sides of the car were narrow lighted openings, each advertised as capable of containing a golf bag.

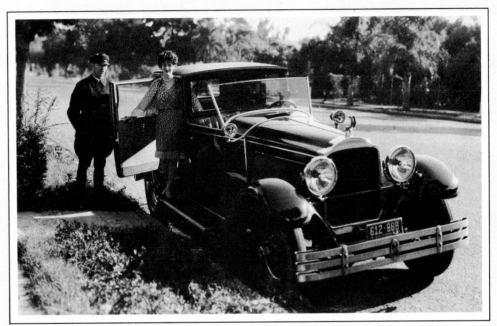

Movie actress Gertrude Olmsted alights from her chauffeured Packard. She designed the car herself.

1929 Packard 6 = 40 Runabout

1928 Hispano-Suiza Cabriolet

Richard Barthelmess takes the wheel of an SSK Mercedes Benz in a scene from the 1930 film, "Son of the Gods."

The Allure of the Import

*Eloquent testimony to the high esteem in which
our products are held is to be gathered from the fact that several
sovereigns, high government officials and similar persons
of exceptional status utilise them year after year.*

MINERVA BROCHURE

In the late '20s, some wealthy Americans began to import European cars of great size and elegance—and cost. As the sales message above illustrates, snob appeal was important; not many people could afford these cars. A French-made Hispano-Suiza cost more than $15,000 in the United States. The Mercedes was comparable in price—and with optional extras might go three times as high. One year singer

Al Jolson bought three; the cheapest ($21,500) was for his wife, Ruby Keeler; a $28,000 town car with gold-plated hardware went to movie mogul Joe Schenck; the cost of the third, which he kept for himself, has been estimated at between $30,000 and $50,000. The Belgian-made Minerva was in the same price range—and if it tended to look a bit dowdy, that was all the better; nobody could take it for anything else.

1926 Minerva Landaulet

Fixing the Horse Highways

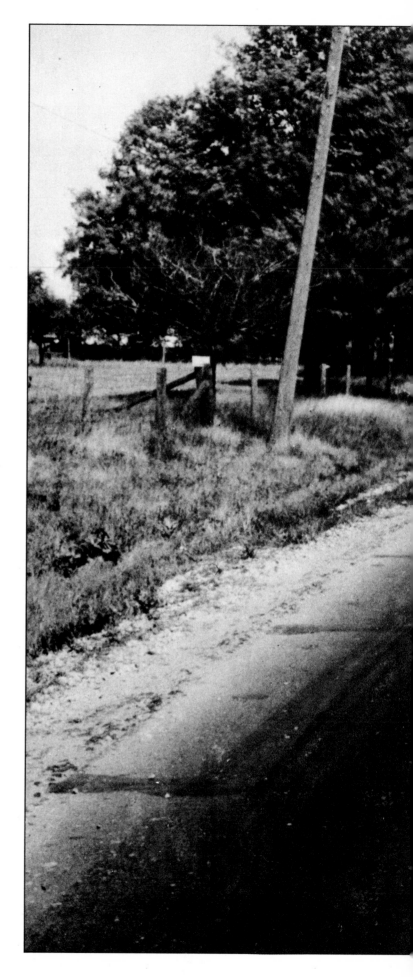

Equipped with an average of three million new cars year-
ly, beguiled by ads to "increase your touring radius," and
raring to go, Americans of the early auto age quickly ran
into a problem: roads. Of the nearly three million miles
of rural highways in 1920, most were still intended for
travel by horse. Of these, only 36,000 had all-weather surfaces that would take the pounding of motor traffic.
Campaigning in 1922 for County Judge of Jackson County, Missouri, a budding politician named Harry Truman
had to ballast his Dodge with bags of cement to keep it
steady on the bumpy road.

As a matter of fact, the problem was political. Away
back in 1838 the federal government began to relinquish
road-building to the states; the states did next to nothing.
In 1893 Congress finally appropriated $10,000 for an Of-
fice of Road Inquiry, and followed up 19 years later with
a $500,000 appropriation, which duly yielded 425 miles
of "improved" roads. Nevertheless, as one highway historian remarks, "U.S. roads were more like those of
Siberia than those of France or England."

But suddenly there were millions of auto drivers—and
they all had votes. As a result, by 1919 all states had highway departments. In 1921 the Federal Highway Act
brought the federal government back into road-building.
Among other results, the new law helped reduce such
anomalies as the hard-surface road in Maine that became
a mud pit when it crossed the line into New Hampshire.
Before the decade's end federal aid was pushing highway
construction at a 10,000-mile-a-year clip.

As traffic problems multiplied, so did breakthroughs
in road construction: the first limited-access road, New
York's Bronx River Parkway, opened in 1923; the first all-
vehicular tunnel—the Holland Tunnel into Manhattan
—was finished in 1927; the first cloverleaf interchange
went into operation at Woodbridge, New Jersey, in 1928.
Of course it was a never-ending cycle: the more the roads
improved, the more they were used. By 1928 the tourist
could drive from New York City to St. Mary's, Kansas, on
paved highways. So he did—and clamored for the government to get going and pave the rest of the way to the coast.

A Michigan Highway Department machine paints a center line down a state road—by now paved and marked for fast-moving auto traffic.

EVERY SHAVER

NOW CAN SNORE

SIX MORE MINUTES

DOES YOUR HUSBAND

MISBEHAVE

GRUNT AND GRUMBLE

THAN BEFORE

BY USING

The Nomad Finds His Way

The multiplying highways that led to beckoning horizons, and the millions of cars built for getting there, required a mundane third factor to make them mesh: road signs. This seemed like such a simple need initially that little attention was paid to it; as a result, by mid-decade America's motorists found themselves looking with puzzlement and dismay at such Rube Goldberg road signs as the one at left showing (among many other things) a detour between Manitowoc and Sheboygan, Wisconsin, on Highway 17. It seemed to require a compass, the skills of celestial navigation and a seer's eye to get where you were going. For years the image of the wandering tourist tussling with unwieldy maps and studying illegible sign boards with a lighted match was good for vaudeville laughs. Another method of route-marking enjoyed a brief vogue: indicating through roads by painting distinctive bands of color on telephone poles, trees and fences along the right of way. Soon, however, there were so many intersecting highways in the East that there weren't enough colors to go around. And in some parts of the West there weren't enough trees and fences to paint.

In 1925 under the authority of the Federal Highway Act of 1921, the Secretary of Agriculture asked the American Association of State Highway Officials to do something about road signs. The result was a system whereby through routes crossing state lines were given either shield-shaped signs identifying them as U.S. highways or circular signs identifying them as state roads. East-west routes were even-numbered, north-south routes odd-numbered and main highways were numbered under 100. Uniform octagonal "Stop" signs, circular "RR Crossing"

signs and diamond "Curve" signs were among the others agreed on. By 1925's end, the signs were going up, the American motorist's ire was going down and—perhaps most important of all—the fast-multiplying service stations found it possible, and smart business, to give away accurate road maps.

Liberated at last, the tourist could look around him at the other signs on the road; what he saw mainly was a clutter of advertising billboards. Most were simply annoying; a few were interesting and instructive. Around Cape Cod and Plymouth, Massachusetts, billboards sited every few miles advertised not codfish or shoes but historic events. In Virginia, every Civil War battlefield was identified by a memorial tablet posted on the adjacent highway.

Among the more pleasurable sights to greet the motorist's eye were the little Burma-Shave signs—a series of six red panels, stuck in the ground along the highway 100 paces apart, each carrying a few words of the complete selling message, usually a bit of humorous doggerel. Dreamed up in 1925 by a literate businessman named Allan Odell, whose family business confronted bankruptcy unless it sold its shaving cream, the jaunty little Burma-Shave signs were first tried out along a pair of Minneapolis roads. Light-hearted, sometimes even iconoclastic, they sold Burma-Shave so well that in 1926 the little clumps of signs began spreading to other regions. The passing motorist, his eyes flicking from one panel to the other as he rode along, got such messages as: "THE 50¢ JAR / SO LARGE / BY HECK / EVEN THE SCOTCH / NOW SHAVE THE NECK / BURMA-SHAVE." Reading these and similar messages the American nomad chuckled and drove on.

RANT AND RAVE?

SHOOT THE BRUTE SOME

As the number of roadside stands climbed into the thousands, Ohio's Health Department warned motorists to "be sure the drinking water is safe."

Motorists, What of the Night?

"Somewhere in these states there is a young man who is going to become rich. He is going to start a chain of small, clean, pleasant hotels, standardized and nationally advertised, along every important motor route in the country. He is not going to waste money on gilt and onyx, but he is going to have agreeable clerks, good coffee, endurable mattresses and good lighting." Thus Sinclair Lewis concluded a *Saturday Evening Post* series of articles on "Adventures in Automobumming."

That was just as the decade started, and Lewis turned out to be a shrewd prophet. In 1920 Americans were hitting the road in huge numbers; no fewer than a million went camping. Housing the new nomads presented a problem—and a challenge. Denver had pioneered in 1919 by opening a 160-acre municipal campsite; the following year 300 cities had municipal camps. By 1923, about 2,000 communities offered camps, some—like that of Los Angeles—boasting cook stoves, laundry tubs and hot water. This was only the beginning. It soon became as clear to small businessmen as it was to Sinclair Lewis that tourists could be a profitable business. Private interests began to supply more substantial—and expensive—accommodations, in the form of tourist courts. Rows and semicircles of little cabins, they were little more than glorified chicken coops when they started, but they prospered and developed; by 1925 the state of Florida registered 178 tourist courts.

The city-owned tourist park in Winona, Minnesota, has the usual amenities including central kitchen facilities, running water and bathrooms.

There also arose the institution of the "tourist home" —the private household that responded to the dual needs of sleepy travelers and scant family exchequer by hanging a sign on the tree by the front doorstep: "Accommodations," or "Tourists Accepted." These establishments varied as widely as the American family itself. Some were comfortable and spotlessly clean; others were not. One weary veteran of sleepless nights mourned: "A Tourist Home by any other name still adds up to a boarding house. The snoring of the occupant of the third floor back isn't art at 3 a.m. Nor is there anything like a symphony in the backfiring barrage put up by those road demons who stomp up the stairs at midnight and depart before dawn."

He concluded gloomily: "Always inspect the bathroom with lights on. Look for that ring around the tub."

The final recourse for the frustrated traveler was the small-town hotel. In 1924 the *Literary Digest* discussed this alternative and voted with Sinclair Lewis. It outlined some of the dimensions of the problem by running this excerpt from a book written by one P. M. Fogg: "Stuffy little rooms, with torn window screens to let the mosquitos in —might as well have no screens at all. One towel—always have to ring for the other five. Soap-cake, big as a minute. And the prices! Scandalous, simply scandalous! Still, it's only once a year, you understand, so what if it does cost a little? One has to keep up a decent appearance."

Filling stations, like this one in New York City, often sold groceries and sandwiches. But the attendant who cleaned a windshield expected a tip.

Motorcycle cops flagged speeders, chased gangsters and escorted notables. These men, attired in varied uniforms, were photographed near San Diego.

3740   JOHN E. WEAVER'S SONS

Rosey's Auto Graveyard near Lancaster, Pennsylvania, displays a few of the millions of cars junked in the '20s—most of them canvas-topped.

The Jazz Age Glossary

The exuberant '20s were extraordinarily fertile years for language in America;

dozens of new words and expressions sprang into existence. Much of the new verbiage was scornful of

established ways; no less than half a dozen of the terms are roughly synonymous words

meaning "nonsense." A partial list of terms that were coined or popularized in the decade appears below.

ALL WET—wrong; arguing a mistaken notion or belief.

APPLESAUCE—a term of derogation; nonsense; same as baloney, bunk, banana oil, hokum and horsefeathers.

BALONEY—nonsense; same as applesauce, etc.

BANANA OIL—nonsense; same as above.

BEE'S KNEES—a superb person or thing.

BELLY LAUGH—a loud, uninhibited laugh.

BERRIES—anything wonderful; similar to bee's knees.

BIBLE BELT—an area in the South or south Midwest where Fundamentalist religion prevails (coined by H. L. Mencken).

BLIND DATE—a date with an unknown person of the opposite sex, usually arranged by a mutual friend.

Dumb Dora

BIG CHEESE—an important person.

BRONX CHEER—a loud derisive noise from an audience (coined by the humorist Bugs Baer, who credited Bronx rooters at athletic events with inventing this mode of expression).

BULL SESSION—an informal group discussion.

BUMP OFF—to murder.

BUNK—nonsense; same as applesauce, etc. (a shortened form of *bunkum*, which is also spelled *buncombe*, from the name of a North Carolina

county whose representative in Congress in 1820 explained the irrelevance of a speech he was making by saying that he was "talking to Buncombe").

Drugstore Cowboy

CAKE-EATER—a ladies' man.

CARRY A TORCH—to suffer from unrequited love.

CAT'S MEOW—anything wonderful; similar to bee's knees, berries.

CHEATERS—eyeglasses.

COPACETIC—excellent.

CRUSH—an infatuation with a person of the opposite sex.

DARB—an excellent person or thing.

DOGS—human feet.

Flapper

DRUGSTORE COWBOY—a fashionably dressed idler who hangs around public places trying to pick up girls.

DUMB DORA—a stupid girl.

FALL GUY—a scapegoat.

FLAPPER—a typical young girl of the '20s, usually with bobbed hair, short skirts and rolled stockings.

FLAT TIRE—a dull, boring person.

FRAME—to cause a person's arrest by giving false evidence.

GAM—a girl's leg (from French dialect *gambe*).

Big Cheese

GATECRASHER—a person who attends a party without an invitation, or a show without paying admission.

GIGGLE WATER—an alcoholic drink.

GIN MILL—a speak-easy.

GOLD DIGGER—a woman who uses feminine charm to extract money from a man.

GOOFY—silly.

GYP—to cheat (from *gypsy*).

HARD-BOILED—tough; without sentiment.

HEEBIE-JEEBIES—the jitters.

HEP—wise.

HIGH-HAT—to snub.

Jalopy

HOKUM—nonsense; same as applesauce, etc.

HOOCH—bootleg liquor (from *Hoochinoo*, a tribe of Alaskan Indians who made distilled liquor).

HOOFER—chorus girl.

Sheik and Sheba

HORSEFEATHERS—nonsense; same as apple-sauce, etc.

HOTSY-TOTSY—pleasing.

JAKE—okay (most commonly used in the phrase "Everything's jake").

JALOPY—an old car.

KEEN—attractive; appealing.

KIDDO—a familiar form of address.

KISSER—the mouth.

LINE—insincere flattery.

LOUNGE LIZARD—a ladies' man; same as cake-eater.

LOUSY—bad; contemptible.

MAIN DRAG—the most important street in a town or city.

Necking

NECK—to caress intimately.

NERTS (NUTS)—an interjection expressing the speaker's disgust.

OSSIFIED—drunk.

PEPPY—full of vitality.

PET—same as neck.

PINCH—to arrest.

PUSHOVER—a person or thing easily overcome.

RASPBERRY—same as Bronx cheer.

RITZY—elegant (from *Ritz*, the Paris hotel).

REAL McCOY, THE—the genuine article (the derivation is in dispute; it comes either from a Scottish clan leader named MacKay; a boxer named Kid McCoy, who had a rival with the same name, or a bootlegger named McCoy who did not adulterate his liquor).

RUN-AROUND—deceptive or delaying action, especially in response to a request.

SCRAM—to leave hurriedly (from *scramble*).

SCREWY—crazy; eccentric.

SEX APPEAL—physical attractiveness to members of the opposite sex.

SHEBA—a young woman with sex appeal.

SHEIK—a young man with sex appeal.

SMELLER—the nose.

SOB SISTER—a woman reporter who leans toward sentimentality in the treatment of her subject matter.

SPEAK-EASY—a saloon or bar selling bootleg whiskey.

SPIFFY—having an elegantly fashionable appearance.

SPIFFLICATED—drunk.

STRUGGLE BUGGY—a car (from its use as a place in which boys tried to seduce girls).

STUCK ON—having a crush on.

SWANKY—ritzy.

SWELL—marvelous.

Hooch

TORPEDO—a hired gunman.

UPCHUCK—to vomit.

WHOOPEE—boisterous, convivial fun.

Picture Credits

The sources for the illustrations which appear in this book are shown below. Credits for the pictures from left to right are separated by semicolons, from top to bottom by dashes.

Fabric design by John R. Martinez.
6,7—Culver Pictures. 8,9—Bostwick-Frohardt Collection owned by KMTV, Omaha. 10,11—Gernsheim Collection, Humanities Research Center, The University of Texas at Austin. 12,13—United Press International. 14,15—G. W. Romer, Miami. 16,17—Caufield & Shook Collection, University of Louisville Photographic Archives. 18,19—Bostwick-Frohardt Collection owned by KMTV, Omaha. 20,21—Courtesy Louise Broecker. 22—Museum of The City of New York; Culver Pictures—Photo World Inc.; United Press International—United Press International; Culver Pictures. 27—United Press International except top right Brown Brothers, bottom right Wide World. 28,29—United Press International. 31—Library of Congress. 32—United Press International(2)—Underwood and Underwood; The Bettmann Archive. 33—State Historical Society of Wisconsin courtesy Charles Scribner's Sons; Underwood and Underwood—Library of Congress; United Press International. 34—Charles Phelps Cushing. 36,37—University of Wisconsin Archives; Collection of Regional History and Cornell University Archives; University of Wisconsin Archives—Minnesota Historical Society; The James Ethiel Boyett Collection. 40,41—Culver Pictures and Sy Seidman. 42,43—Missouri Historical Society. 44,45—Brown Brothers. 46,47—Culver Pictures. 48—Brown Brothers. 50—From *Life*, March 3, 1927. 51—Nickolas Muray. 52—Culver Pictures; from *Life*, January 13, 1927—from *Life*, August 26, 1926; from *Life*, November 19, 1925. 53—From *Life*, June 3, 1926. 54—From *Life*, January 29, 1925; from *Life*, August 20, 1925—from *Life*, December 1927. 55—From *Life*, June 14, 1928. 56,57—From *Life*, December 9, 1926. 58,59—Courtesy Airportworld Magazine. 61—Culver Pictures. 62—U.S. Air Force. 63—Minnesota Historical Society. 64,65—United Press International. 66,67—Bostwick-Frohardt Collection owned by KMTV, Omaha; United States Post Office Department. 68—Transworld Airlines. 69—Pan American World Airways. 70—Burton Historical Collection, Detroit Public Library; Ford Archives, Henry Ford Museum, Dearborn, Michigan—United Air Lines; Pan American World Airways—United Air Lines; Burton Historical Collection, Detroit Public Library. 71—Burton Historical Collection, Detroit Public Library. 72—Western Airlines. 74,75—Burton Historical Collection, Detroit Public Library. 76,77—*Jazzmen*/Ramsey Archive. 79—Photo Files. 80,81—Paul Edward Miller. 82—Photo Files. 83—From *A Pictorial History of Jazz* by Orrin Keepnews and Bill Grauer Jr., Crown Publishers, 1966. 84,85—Photo Files—from *Jazz, The New York Scene*, Record Research Archives, courtesy Len Kunstadt; Ernest Smith Collection; Photo Files—no credit; *Jazz, The New York Scene*, Record Research Archives, courtesy Len Kunstadt. 86,87—Photo Files. 88,89—Courtesy Frank Driggs and Ben M. Hall. 90—Edward Steichen, Collection The Museum of Modern Art, New York. 92,93—Culver Pictures. 94,95—Wide World. 97—From *Life*, September 22, 1921. 98,99—The Smithsonian Institution. 100,101—Brown Brothers. 102,103—Brown Brothers(2); Culver Pictures—courtesy Irving Settel; Underwood and Underwood. 104—Culver Pictures; Lebhar-Friedman Publications Inc.—MacDonald Photos courtesy Edholm and Blomgren, Lincoln, Nebraska; Bostwick-Frohardt Collection owned by KMTV, Omaha—Lebhar-Friedman Publications Inc.(2)—Historical Collection Title Insurance and Trust Company, San Diego; MacDonald Photos courtesy Edholm and Blomgren, Lincoln, Nebraska. 105—Lebhar-Friedman Publications Inc.(2)—MacDonald Photos courtesy Edholm and Blomgren, Lincoln, Nebraska(2). 106—From *The Best Remaining Seats* by Ben M. Hall. 107—Collection Ben M. Hall. 108,109,110—Henry Groskinsky. 111—From *The Best Remaining Seats* by Ben M. Hall. 112,113—Minnesota Historical Society. 114—United Press International. 116—Underwood and Underwood; Culver Pictures. 117—United Press International; Brown Brothers. 119—The Bettmann Archive. 120—Culver Pictures; no credit—Culver Pictures; from *Life*, June 13, 1930. 121—From *Life*, September 13, 1929; Sy Seidman—from *Life*, May 17, 1929; Culver Pictures. 122—Culver Pictures. 123—No credit. 124—Culver Pictures except bottom right from *Life*, October 11, 1923. 125,126,127—Culver Pictures. 129—© The New York Times 1929. 130,131—The New York Times. 132,133—From the collection of the late Mario Cavagnaro. 135—Nickolas Muray. 136—United Press International. 137—Brown Brothers. 138—Culver Pictures. 139—United Press International. 140,141—Brown Brothers; United Press International; Culver Pictures. 142—Miami Beach News Service. 143—Culver Pictures. 144,145—Bert Morgan. 146—Culver Pictures. 147—Brown Brothers. 148 to 151—Culver Pictures. 152,153—United Press International. 155—*The Detroit News*. 156—Drawing by G. Price, copr. © 1928, 1956 The New Yorker Magazine Inc.; drawing by Peter Arno, copr. © 1928, 1956 The New Yorker Magazine Inc.—drawing by I. Klein, copr. © 1927, 1955 The New Yorker Magazine Inc. 157—Drawing by Bohanan copr. © 1927, 1955 The New Yorker Magazine Inc.; Culver Pictures—Museum of the City of New York; Sy Seidman. 158—Underwood and Underwood. 159—Library of Congress except top left Culver Pictures. 161—From FORTUNE June 1933, painting by Pierre Brissaud. 162—California Historical Society; New York Historical Society (2)—New York Historical Society; Herb Orth(2) Courtesy Detroit Historical Museum—New York Historical Society(3)—Herb Orth(3) Courtesy Detroit Historical Museum—Herb Orth, courtesy Sy Seidman; New York Historical Society (2)—Herb Orth, courtesy Detroit Historical Society(2); Sy Seidman(1). 163—United Press International. 164—Underwood and Underwood; California Historical Society, San Francisco. 165—Museum of the City of New York; Courtesy Pabst Brewing Co. 167—Underwood and Underwood. 168,169—Gernsheim Collection, Humanities Research Center, The University of Texas at Austin. 170—From *Life*, August 3, 1922. 171—United Press International. 172,173—Cincinnati Public Library. 174—United Press International except top row center and 2nd row left Chicago Daily News, 2nd row center Wide World. 178,179—Collection of Frank Rogers and Son. 181—From *Life*, October 4, 1929. 182—From *Life*, June 28, 1929; from *Life*, April 26, 1929—from *Life*, May 10, 1929; from *Life*, September 6, 1929. 183—From *Life*, July 19, 1929; from *Life*, July 12, 1929—From *Life*, June 21, 1929; from *Life*, August 30, 1929. 185—© The New York *Daily News*. 186,187—United Press International. 188—Wide World courtesy The New York Times. 189—United Press International except top right Wide World. 190—Wide World; United Press International (2)—The New York *Daily News*. 191—Wide World except inset United Press International. 192—Harry Grogin. 193—Harry Grogin—United Press International. 194—Los Angeles Times—Wide World. 195—Wide World—Culver Pictures. 196—Brown Brothers. 197—United Press International. 198—United Press International. 199—United Press International except top left The New York Daily News. 200—Library of Congress except center Culver Pictures (2). 202, 203—Reproduced by permission of the owner. 205—Nickolas Muray. 206—Culver Pictures except top left Nickolas Muray. 209—Culver Pictures. 210—Edward Steichen, collection The Museum of Modern Art. 213,214,217—Nickolas Muray. 219—Underwood and Underwood. 220—Culver Pictures. 221—United Press International. 222,223—Library of Congress. 224—Underwood and Underwood. 225—Brown Brothers. 228 to 232—Culver Pictures. 233—Culver Pictures—The Museum of Modern Art/Film Stills Archive. 234—Culver Pictures except top right The Museum of Modern Art/Film Stills Archive. 235—Culver Pictures—The Bettmann Archive; The Museum of Modern Art/Film Stills Archive. 236-237—Culver Pictures except top left The Museum of Modern Art/Film Stills Archive. 238, 239—United Press International. 241—United Press International. 242,243—Underwood and Underwood. 244—Brown Brothers. 245—The Sunpapers, Baltimore. 246,247—United Press International. 248,249—Collection of Frank Rogers and Son. 250—Brown Brothers. 251—United Press International. 252—Culver Pictures. 253—Brown Brothers. 254,255—Michigan Historical Commission. 257—Henry Austin Clark Jr., The Long Island Automotive Museum, Southampton. 258,259—Henry Austin Clark Jr., The Long Island Automotive Museum, Southampton, except top Brown Brothers. 260,261—George A. Moffitt—Henry Austin Clark Jr., The Long Island Automotive Museum, Southampton(2). 262,263—Culver Pictures—Henry Austin Clark Jr., The Long Island Automotive Museum, Southampton(2). 264,265—Henry Austin Clark Jr., The Long Island Automotive Museum, Southampton—Culver Pictures; Detroit Public Library Automotive History Collection. 266,267—Michigan Historical Commission. 268—State Historical Society of Wisconsin. 270,271—Brown Brothers. 272,273—Minnesota Historical Society. 274,275—Brown Brothers. 276, 277—Historical Collection, Title Insurance & Trust Company, San Diego. 278,279—Culver Pictures. 280—From *Life*, June 3, 1926; no credit—courtesy Mrs. John Held Jr.; from *Life*, January 4, 1929. 281—From *Life*, September 6, 1928—from *Life*, September 22, 1927; *Life*, November 23, 1928; from *Life*, April 22, 1926.

Acknowledgments

The editors of this book wish to thank the following persons and institutions for their assistance:

The Academy of Motion Picture Arts and Sciences, Hollywood; Sid Albright, Information Bureau Manager, Western Airlines; Natalie Andrews, Assistant, Photographic Archives, University of Louisville; Frances Bearden, Fondren Library, Southern Methodist University; Jerry Berns, "21" Club, New York; Amelia D. Bielaski, Curator, Smith-Telfer Collection, New York State Historical Association, Cooperstown, New York; The Boeing Company, Seattle; Paul Bonner Jr., The Condé Nast Publications Inc., New York; Margery Booker, Chamber of Commerce, San Francisco; Larry Booth, Director of Historical Collection, Title Insurance and Trust Company, San Diego; James J. Bradley, Automotive History Collection, Detroit Public Library; Ruth P. Braun, *The Detroit News*, Detroit; Henry Austin Clark Jr., Long Island Automotive Museum, Southampton; Mrs. Robert Crowe, Playa del Rey, California; Virginia Daiker, Prints and Photographs Division, Library of Congress; Alice Dalligan, Curator of Manuscripts, Burton Historical Collection, Detroit Public Library; James Davis, Librarian, Western History Department, Denver Public Library; Leslie R. Diveley, Columbia, Missouri; Frank Driggs, New York; Edholm and Blomgren, Photographers, Lincoln, Nebraska; Ruth K. Field, Curator of Pictures, Missouri Historical Society, St. Louis; Hannah D. French, Wellesley College Library, Wellesley, Massachusetts; Estelle Galbreath, Piggly Wiggly Corporation, Jacksonville, Florida; Dorothy Gimmestad, Acting Curator, Picture Department, Minnesota Historical Society, St. Paul; Henry Graham, San Antonio; Ben Hall, New York; Gita Hall, Warner-Lambert Pharmaceutical Company, New York; Dale Hoaglan, KMTV, Omaha; Orrin Keepnews, Milestone Records, New York; Dick Lemen, East Moline, Illinois; David Lighthall, editor, *Chainstore Age*, New York; Ed Matthews, Piggly Wiggly Corporation, Jacksonville, Florida; Jo and Fred Mazulla, Denver; Robert D. Monroe, Chief of Special Collections, University of Washington Library, Seattle; Joseph E. Molloy, Librarian, *Philadelphia Inquirer*, Philadelphia; Mrs. Nickolas Muray, New York; Daniel Murphy, Leslie Jones Collection, *The Boston Herald*, Boston; Museum of the City of New York; Kathleen Pierson, State Historical Society of Colorado, Denver; Victor R. Plukas, Bank Historian, Security Pacific National Bank, Los Angeles; Ruth Revels, Local History Department, Milwaukee Public Library; Norman Rogers, Dallas; Gleason Wait Romer, Miami; Meyer Rosen, News Bureau Chief, *Los Angeles Times*, Los Angeles; Winthrop Sears Jr., Henry Ford Museum, Dearborn, Michigan; Irving Settel, New York; Bertha Stratford, Museum of History and Industry, Seattle; Ray Stuart, Hollywood, California; Patrick Sullivan, Library of the Commonwealth of Massachusetts, Boston; Judith Topaz, Assistant, Iconographic Collections, State Historical Society of Wisconsin, Madison; Mary Wotring, Head of Archives, Columbia Records, New York.

Bibliography

Abels, Jules, *In the Time of Silent Cal*. G. P. Putnam's Sons, 1969.

Allen, Frederick Lewis, *Only Yesterday*. Harper & Row, 1964.

Asbury, Herbert, *The Great Illusion*.
    Doubleday & Company, Inc., 1950.

Bird, Caroline, *The Invisible Scar*. David McKay Co., 1966.

Borgeson, Griffith and Jaderquist, Eugene, *Sports and Classic Cars*.
    Prentice-Hall, 1955.

Churchill, Allen, *Remember When*. Golden Press, Inc., 1967.

Clutton, Cecil and Stanford, John, *The Vintage Motor-Car*.
    Charles Scribner's Sons, 1955.

Daniels, Jonathan, *The Time Between the Wars*.
    Doubleday & Company, 1966.

Danzig, Allison and Brandwein, Peter, eds., *Sport's Golden Age*.
    Harper & Brothers, 1948.

Dulles, Foster R., *Twentieth Century America*. Houghton Mifflin Co., 1945.

Earnest, Ernest, *Academic Procession*. The Bobbs-Merrill
    Company, Inc., 1953.

Franklin, Joe, *Classics of the Silent Screen*. The Citadel Press, 1959.

Galbraith, John Kenneth, *The Great Crash: 1929*.
    Houghton Mifflin Co., 1955.

Hall, Ben M., *The Best Remaining Seats*. Clarkson N. Potter, Inc., 1961.

Harriman, Margaret Chase, *The Vicious Circle*. Rinehart & Company, 1951.

Johnston, Alva, *The Legendary Mizners*. Farrar, Straus and Young, 1953.

Merz, Charles, *The Dry Decade*. Doubleday, Doran & Company, 1931.

Ramsey, Frederick Jr. and Smith, Charles E., eds., *Jazzmen*.
    Harcourt, Brace, 1939.

Russell, Francis, *The Shadow of Blooming Grove*.
    McGraw-Hill Book Co., 1968.

Sann, Paul, *Fads, Follies and Delusions of the American People*.
    Crown Publishers, Inc., 1967.
    The Lawless Decade. Crown Publishers, Inc., 1957.

Settel, Irving, *A Pictorial History of Radio*. Grossett & Dunlap, 1967.

Shapiro, Nat and Hentoff, Nat, eds., *Hear Me Talkin' To Ya*. Rinehart &
    Co., 1955.

Sinclair, Andrew, *Prohibition, The Era of Excess*.
    Little, Brown and Company, 1962.

Slosson, Preston W., *The Great Crusade and After: 1914-1928*.
    The Macmillan Company, 1930.

Stevenson, Elizabeth, *Babbitts and Bohemians: The American 1920s*.
    The Macmillan Company, 1967.

Sullivan, Mark, *Our Times. Vol. 6, The Twenties*.
    Charles Scribner's Sons, 1937.

Walker, Stanley, *The Night Club Era*. Frederick A. Stokes Company, 1933.

Wood, James P., *The Story of Advertising*. Ronald Press Co., 1958.

Text Credits

26—Lippmann quote from *A Preface to Morals* by Walter Lippmann. Macmillan Co., 1929, p. 17. 45—Fitzgerald, from *Thalberg* by Bob Thomas. Doubleday & Company, Inc. 1969, p. 105. 49—Fitzgerald on New York from *Scott Fitzgerald* by Andrew Turnbull. Charles Scribner's Sons, 1962, p. 183. 101—De Forest quote from *The Story of Advertising* by James Playsted Wood. The Ronald Press Company, 1958, p. 414. 113—Prayer for businessmen from the *American Mercury*, "Americana" column. April 1929. 115—From *The Man Nobody Knows* by Bruce Barton. The Bobbs-Merrill Company, copyright 1924, copyright renewed 1952 by Bruce Barton. Reprinted by permission of Bruce Barton heirs. 146—Rice, from *New York Sun*, September 29, 1930. Keeler, from *Yesterday in Sports*, ed. by John Durant. A.S. Barnes and Company, 1956, pp. 99-100. 160—From *The Night Club Era* by Stanley Walker. Frederick A. Stokes Company, 1933, pp. 288-289. 166—Einstein, from *Prohibition Agent No. 1* by Izzy Einstein. Frederick A. Stokes Company, 1932, p. 14. 208 —"Eel-Grass," "First Fig" and "Feast":From *Collected Poems* by Edna St. Vincent Millay, edited by Norma Millay. Harper & Row Publishers, pp. 68, 127, 158. Copyright 1921, 1922, 1923; renewed 1948, 1950, 1951. Used by permission of Norma Millay Ellis. 211—"Democratic man": Copyright 1926 and renewed 1954 by H. L. Mencken. Reprinted from *The Vintage Mencken*, Gathered by Alistair Cooke, by permission of Alfred A. Knopf, Inc., p. 175—"A boy" and "Sin": From *The Vintage Mencken*, Gathered by Alistair Cooke. Copyright 1955 by Alfred A. Knopf, Inc., pp. 183, 187-188. Reprinted by permission of the publisher. 212—"Cabaret," "Lament for Dark Peoples" and "Afraid": From *The Weary Blues* by Langston Hughes. Copyright 1926 and renewed 1954 by Langston Hughes. Reprinted by permission of Alfred A. Knopf, Inc., pp. 29, 100, 101. 215—From *O'Neill and His Plays* edited by Oscar Cargill, N.B. Fagin and W.J. Fisher. New York University Press, 1961, pp. 104 and 106. 216—From *Babbitt* by Sinclair Lewis. Copyright 1922 by Harcourt, Brace & World Inc.; renewed 1950 by Sinclair Lewis, pp. 42-43. Reprinted by permission of publishers.

Index

Numbers in italics indicate an illustration of the subject mentioned.

Printed in U.S.A.

61190

E
161
T55
vol.3

OVERSIZE
TIME-LIFE BOOKS
    THIS FABULOUS CENTURY.

DATE DUE

MAR 30 1995	
APR 22 1995	
NOV 16 1997	
NOV 30 1997	
FEB 08 1999	
MAR 15 2000	
MAY 07 2001	
DEC 06 2004	
APR 12 2005	
DEC 14 2005	
MAY 10 2007	
OCT 19 2011	